21 ways of Being *Happy*

SHAMA PATEL

GRAPEVINE INDIA

Grapevine India Publishers Pvt. Ltd.
Plot No.4, First Floor
Pandav Nagar
Opposite Shadipur Metro Station
Patel Nagar
New Delhi - 110008
India

grapevineindiapublishers@gmail.com
contact@grapevineindia.com

Printed and bound in New Delhi

Oh soul,
You worry too much.
You have seen your own strength.
You have seen your own beauty.
You have seen your golden wings.
Of anything less,
Why do you worry?
You are in truth
The soul, of the soul, of the soul.

~ Rumi

ACKNOWLEDGMENT

I want to begin this section of gratitude by thanking that Supreme Intelligence, without whose blessings I wouldn't have been what I am today. I am most grateful to Him for giving me a life and the ability to endure and cherish my existence. This book is His blessing and I owe it to Him.

My gratitude list ought to start with the mention of the man who is behind this concept and whose trust in me and my writing led me to create 21 beautiful ways of being happy – Sachin Garg. I thank him for believing in me and being a wonderful friend and mentor throughout this journey. I am grateful to Grapevine Publications and team for creating a motivating platform for budding writers like me. I am most thankful to my editor Ashna Banga who patiently altered all my errors and helped me give this script a beautiful form. Special gratitude goes out to Chandni Dua for bringing in her creative energies and creating a gorgeously perfect cover for this book.

I do believe in the existence of Guardian Angels and in my life, Shamira Pujani has been one of those special angels who held me close when life seemed tough, and laughed by my side when the same life seemed the most beautiful thing to live. I owe my saneness as well as (a little) insaneness to her.

My journey would definitely be incomplete without

my wonderful parents, Arif Patel and Zeenat Patel, who always encouraged me to pursue my dreams and stood by me every single moment of my life. They are the two most gracious souls any child could wish to have as parents. My gorgeous sister Heena Patel completes this special bond I call Family. She is my biggest strength and also my prime weakness. This feeling of gratitude extends to two of the most beautiful ladies in my life, who readily shower their special blessings on me – My Dadi and Nanima.

I am blessed to have some of the most pure, beautiful and blessed souls around who never let go of a chance to love me, encourage me and make me feel like the most special person on this planet – Siraj Ali Gilani, Raziya Bhayani, Amit Bhayani, Sehul Shah, Shabina Masani, Sharmeen Bhiwani, Asif Ali Sayani, Nadia Sayani, Asif Panjwani, Sabina Dosani, Azhar Lakhani, Saurabh Vyas, Shazia Merchant, Moaiz Gilani, Ruhi Kathane, Shikha Saraf, Gaurav Gite and Manav Verma.

My special love and gratitude goes out to my two precious children – Shifa Bhiwani and Ryan Bhayani for bringing me closer to loving the precious gift of universe called Life.

To all my cousins, well-wishers and readers, I will always be grateful to you for all your love and support.

"If a man told God that he wanted most of all to help the suffering world, no matter the price to himself, and God answered and told him what he must do, should the man do as he is told?"

"Of course, Master!" cried the many. "It should be pleasure for him to suffer the tortures of hell itself, should God ask it!"

"No matter what those tortures, or how difficult the task?" "Honor to be hanged, glory to be nailed to a tree and burned, if so be that God has asked," said they.

"And what would you do," the Master said unto the multitude (the crowd), "If God spoke directly to your face and said...

"I command that you be happy in the world, as long as you live! What would you do then?"

And the multitude was silent, not a voice, not a sound was heard upon the hillsides, across the valleys where they stood...

~ Richard Bach
(ILLUSIONS - The Adventures of a Reluctant Messiah)

***

CONTENTS

Introduction to Happiness!

Often in therapy, I have clients who come to me with major emotional issues and with a hope that I will have the answers to all their unanswered questions. Since I am no God, I tell them that I don't have direct answers to their questions, but I can help them ease out the stress that is building around in the process of finding those answers. Some clients have a direct agenda in the counselling sessions – "I want to be happy in life. Tell me what to do" or "I want to feel more positive in life. Tell me what to do". Before we get talking and exploring these questions, there comes a condition - "But… I am very busy with my work, family and other commitments so I don't have much time, you see! Can you give me a quick fix?" I smile at them and say, "Let's take one thing at a time…" and begin my counselling sessions.

As human beings, we are forever running. Running towards a better self, better opportunities, a better future, better life, more comfort and luxuries, and in this process of running towards the non-existent future, there comes a time when we feel tired and worn out. That's when we feel the need to slow down, the need to relax. Even though we feel tired, some of us continue to run until our body begins to take the toll. We desire everything in our lives that can make our existence 'picture perfect' and we want it at a lightning speed. When I get such clients who are in haste to figure out everything about life, I consciously take the first ten minutes to calm them down. The human mind is so accustomed to getting everything at a click that it wants to follow the same process for experiencing peace and happiness. We don't have time to calm down but we want to feel happy and at peace while we continue to run the rat race. We conveniently expect someone else to know on our behalf where can we find happiness. In the rush to reach that blissful state, we often negate the fact that 'happiness' is a very relative term. What brings me happiness may not necessarily be the thing that can bring happiness to someone else. Secondly, we are never satisfied and happy with one thing. The list starts with one and continues to multiply with each passing day.

I have had clients say - "I am so disturbed right now! I hate my job and the politics that people play at my office. I just hope and pray I get a different job and I am sure I will be happy then." While some do feel happy once they get a new job, others continue to extend the 'happiness' list by saying – "If only my package increases by 12%, I will be happy", "If I get a work-from-home permit, I will be satisfied with my job" or "if I get to go off site to Australia, I will be happy". The list of 'moments of being happy' never really ends.

We often tend to attach happiness with an event which is likely to happen in the near future and in the desire to reach that place, we let go of the preset joys which are with us in the moment. Then there is the other breed who believes that happiness is sold in shops in the form of alcohol, clothes, cigarettes, drugs, shoes, gadgets and so on. They declare that they derive happiness from these provisions and yet they are the ones who sit in a corner a few days later and wonder, "Where is my life going? What should I do to make my life better and happier?"

While we all have our own list of what gives us happiness, sometimes it becomes necessary to stop looking at the list on a superficial level and make a list of things that helps us connect with the 'happiness' within and stay with the feeling for a longer time. When I got fed up of finding happiness in all the materialistic things around me, I decided to explore other authentic ways that can make me or any other person happy. And by the word 'happy', I mean the ability to love and live life in peace every single minute of consciousness. While it took me years of personal search and professional practice to list these 21 ways, it also took me years of practice to experience each one of them! Finding these ways definitely did not make me a '*Guruma* of Happiness', neither did it confirm that henceforth I will not have any worries in my life. What it did help me with was that it got me closer to myself. It helped me find peace in the chaotic life which I still continue to live. It made me fall in love with myself and that belief in myself gave me courage to sustain every challenge thrown my way.

I hope that these 21 ways will help you smile more and appreciate goodness in life! Who knows you may be able to add 21 more ways to this list and contribute in spreading this happiness bug around, because there aren't just 21 ways but more than 2001 ways of seeking and sustaining happiness. It is up to you to find the one that brings you inner peace and joy, and fills your life with ecstasy.

1 Know Thyself

"He who knows others is wise; he who knows himself is enlightened."

~ Lao Tzu

Many *rishi munis* and sages have experienced the journey towards inner self and have regarded that as a source of knowledge and a way to attain *nirvana*. While our ancient scriptures also talk about the inward journey, it is often believed in society that people who wish to go on a spiritual search are the only ones who should follow this path. For a common man, which here means the one who isn't willing to give up the materialistic world to achieve spiritual enlightenment, the journey towards self has always remained an alien concept.

Right from childhood we are taught to be good to others, to value others' needs, to love and care for others and in order to make the other person happy, we travel an extra mile to know everything about them – likes, dislikes, favourite color, favourite dish and so on. Especially when it comes to a romantic relationship, couples usually begin with showering bucket full of love on each other. They often go out of their way to know every single detail about the other and make sure that they are updated with every aspect of their partner's life. So when the other person seems to know so much about them, they stop remembering things about themselves. More often than not, we seem to have all the time in this world to get to know someone else better but the mere idea of knowing our self better sounds too weird to actualize and we certainly don't seem to have time for it.

A 68 year old lady once came to me for counselling to overcome the fear she had developed over the last few years. She complained of obsessive thinking and constant fear of death and anxiety when she is left alone at home. In the course of therapy, I began to explore her life as a child, a single parent and a widow. When I asked what she loves about herself, she stared at me for a while, trying to understand if I was actually serious. Slowly, she responded, "I don't know. Well, there are a lot of things about me which I don't like. But what I love about myself? I don't know."

"It's OK. Take your time. I am sure there must be something," I encouraged.

"Well, I am a good mother. At least that's what my son says," she said.

"OK. That's a good start! We have one thing from nothing. Let's try and list down some more."

"Umm... I was a good employee as my boss always praised me for my work. I am a religious person because I go to church regularly and pray. My tuition children used to say I am a good teacher so I take it that I am good at teaching. Though I was very strict as well and I am usually very demanding..." Saying so, she unconsciously jumped from listing the good things to listing the not-so-good things about her and each time she did that, I had to bring the focus back to what she loved about herself. She listed every possible thing that others had told her was good about her. She blindly believed all of it – both good and bad self reviews. She was habitual of looking at herself from others' eyes.

That day, the lady told me, "I can't believe I let go of my 68 years of life not spending time knowing myself. About knowing what I loved to do and doing it. About taking care of myself and being there for myself. Maybe that's why now when I need help, I immediately begin to look for someone around. I can't handle my own self. I can't believe that it's today, after so many years, that I am sitting and making a list of what I think I love about myself!" I smiled at her and told her at least she has started the journey and that's what matters! She confessed that she was getting these thrills of knowing someone she has never known and she was happy and looking forward to this self-discovery. She spent more than half of her life becoming a good daughter, an efficient wife, a mother, a good citizen and all this to make someone else feel better. In doing so, she never found time to know herself beyond these identities and once these identities or these roles took a backset or ceased to exist, life suddenly seemed unrecognizable to her. The only way to recognize it and be happy was to break the ice with her 'self'.

To know yourself means to spend time looking beyond your worldly identities. It's about getting to understand yourself better – what is it that you love to do; what it is that you dislike doing; what are your strengths and weaknesses (your innate qualities, not the people around); what brings you joy; knowing your mood swings and finding the cause for the same; understanding what upsets you more or what triggers your anger; knowing what brings you peace; finding ways to calm yourself when you are under stress; knowing your beliefs and values and understanding why do you believe in it! All these ways of introspection get you closer to the person who you are, so that the next time you are asked a question like - "Dude! Why are you so angry and pissed?" you would have something real to say.

It's important to know yourself so that you always have a reliable person around – yourself. That urge of constantly leaning on someone else's shoulder, that craving of having someone else to love you and pamper you often makes you feel like a loner.

So when you trust yourself, you learn to hold on to your own strengths and the focus is then brought from the outside to the inside. And that's when you will experience the thrill of knowing yourself better than someone else, and you can take pride in your self-worth.

This brings us to another situation we all face. A low self-worth, often brought about by people surrounding us who make us feel that we are good for nothing. If you don't succeed academically, you are regarded as a dumb kid; you fail to get a good job, you are called a loser; you fail to get married at the right age, you are labeled as hopeless. No matter what you do to 'fit in', you are left feeling rotten and unwanted. When you begin this journey of knowing yourself, you understand that you are not a bad person if you fail your exam or don't get a high paying job or fail to find a perfect match. You begin to love and embrace yourself in the worst possible situation and that is when you learn to start feeling worthwhile. You begin to learn that you are a wonderful person even if you feel your life is screwed up. And in the moments when you feel nobody understands you or nobody cares for you, your 'self' will become capable of giving you that warm hug and a shoulder to lean on!

Ways to get to know yourself:

Begin with standing in front of a mirror and giving yourself a smile - it does sound funny and ridiculous but do it anyway. Bring a pen and a diary and start creating lists as mentioned below:

- Write down what you love about yourself: Let the voice be your own rather than something that echoes the voice of your parents, friends, lover or ex.
- What makes you happy and what makes you crappy.
- Your fears, weaknesses and strengths: Qualities such as willpower, intelligence, hard work etc classify as strengths, while tardiness, procrastination, impatience etc can be called weaknesses. Don't list down names of people here. This is only about you.
- What ticks you off: Focus more on situations versus your feelings rather than listing down names of annoying people.

- Know what makes you feel alive: Focus more on instances and feelings.
- Title the page 'Who am I' and discover one thing - positive or negative - about yourself each day and keep adding to the list.

Revisit this list when you feel confused about anything. You'd be surprised at how well you start adding things to it as you gradually start focusing on understanding yourself.

While you are busy listing these things, you might feel you are wasting time, your mind will constantly remind you of other 'important things' to do, but remind yourself that knowing yourself is more important. It will help generate the love, trust, confidence and courage which you thought you never had!

The next time someone asks you - "Who are you?" - you would have a whole encyclopedia of yourself and would feel happy that you didn't have to wait for seventy years to be introduced to the person you really are and the only one who can bring you unconditional love and happiness!

2 | Love Yourself

You cannot be lonely if you like the person you're alone with.

~ Wayne Dyer

"I can't stay alone," said one of my clients in a therapy session.

"OK. What happens when you are alone?"

"I start getting anxious. I start calling my friends. I usually hang out with them till late at night so that I just have to come home and sleep. I often have trouble falling asleep. I just can't sit alone in a room especially when I don't have any work to do. And then, just to kill time, I start smoking back to back."

Dhanesh got hooked to smoking and began to lose interest in his personal and professional life. He concluded that his life is a total waste and that it is easy to end it than living in the unbearable circumstances every single day. His anxiety was intensified before he decided to seek therapy, and to reduce his stress, he regarded cigarette smoking as the best and most convenient option. Unfortunately, smoking is one of the most common defence mechanisms[1]. He developed severe bronchitis infection at a very young age.

In the course of therapy, I found out that Dhanesh was sexually abused as a child and that memory which he thought he had forgotten about was still alive in his subconscious mind. In such traumatic episodes, people usually feel that they have overcome the past and have moved on, but what we fail to understand is that while we are experiencing that trauma, we tend to form conclusions in our head which remain with us, only to be shattered when we have another such experience. Dhanesh told me he hates himself as a person. He strongly believed that he is born to fail in everything he does and everyone around him takes advantage of him all the time. He was convinced that how much ever he works hard, he will never to able to live a happy life.

I asked him, "Do you blame yourself for what happened to you as a child? Do you feel you could have said no to it or would have fought against it and curse yourself for not doing that?"

"Sometimes. Yes. I am a man and I am supposed to fight it out and I don't know how I didn't."

"Have you been able to forgive yourself for it?"

"I can't. How can I? I let that happen and because I did, I should pay for the consequences, right?"

"Wrong. You were nine when it started. Even if you wanted to, it would have been difficult for you to protect yourself because the person involved was much stronger than you. You did not have anybody's support and you were afraid of telling your family because of the fear of being abandoned and the whole idea of shame that you let your family down. You were a child then! What happened then is not your fault. But now, you are an adult. You are in a position to fight back and take charge of your life. You are no more vulnerable when you are alone. You need to forgive yourself for what happened to you when you were most vulnerable."

It took us several counselling sessions to help Dhanesh make peace with himself. The guilt of letting his family down was so much that he kept finding flaws in him and believing that he isn't worthy of any goodness or happiness. It was unbelievable how tough it was for him to stop hating and start loving himself.

We often carry emotional baggage about 'self' and secretly begin to define ourselves at each stage of our life. Sometimes we hear the voice inside us telling how good we are and sometimes the same voice belittles us to such an extent that we start hating ourselves. The experiences we have as a child leave us with certain beliefs that get imprinted in us for a lifetime. This self-judgment usually defines our relationship with ourselves. Example, if a person is constantly criticized in his growing years or if he has had parents who believe that the child 'should'/'must' excel in every field, he is more likely to grow up and develop a self-critical voice that will make him believe that he will never be good enough!

To add to this, right from the time we are born, we are never left alone. In our growing years, we have parents who constantly kept an eye on us to make sure we feel their presence all the time because when we are young, being/staying alone is considered to be risky and scary. The mind gets conditioned to believe that being alone leads to physical or emotional damage and hence, you must always seek external support, even if that support is way more risky than yourself. So when there's a situation where a person has to be alone, he/she experiences automated anxiety, fear and restlessness. The mind becomes alert and starts throwing warning signs like 'something isn't right' or 'something bad may happen'. Sometimes these signs are in the form of feelings more than thoughts - loneliness, shame, guilt, pain, agitation etc. You begin to feel fearful and uneasy from within. This is nothing but your mind relating the situation in your past, where you were small and dependent, and connecting it with the illusionary future.

Since nobody taught us what to do or how to be happy when we are alone, we feel lost. And while we are alone, the only thing we have learnt to do is to sit and criticize ourselves. So firstly, we aren't taught the concept of 'being alone and being happy' and secondly, we are conditioned to be self-critical when we are left alone! The resulting feeling in such a situation is bound to be of self-hatred or self-detachment.

A client once told me that she loves herself as a person. I acknowledged that and asked her, "What is it that you don't love about yourself?" and the list to this question went beyond expectations! Right from the physical features to eating habits to lack of creative genes, she was determined to change maximum things about her if given a chance. So I explained to her the meaning of 'loving yourself'.

When you embrace the positive as well as the negative part of you as a whole, that's when you begin the journey of falling in love with self. When you stop finding flaws in yourself and stop making efforts in turning yourself into some other person who you wish to be, you begin to fall in love with yourself. When you stop changing every single thing about you which some other person hates or when you stop changing the good things in you because your lover did not like that about you, you begin the process of loving yourself.

To love yourself is to accept yourself the way you are – fat, thin, dark, fair, tall, short, intelligent, dumb whatever you are, you are your person. To love yourself is to embrace that person in you with all your heart and mind just the way you embrace your lover. The feeling that you feel for them is exactly what needs to be felt by you for your 'self'. And the moment you begin to feel this inward love, is the moment when you begin to relax and feel at peace in your own company. You stop feeling anxious when you are left alone and you no longer feel dependent on someone else to make you feel good.

While taking this up with another client, I was asked, "But isn't loving your 'self' the same as being a narcissist?"

Wikipedia defines narcissism as 'the pursuit of gratification from vanity, or egotistic admiration of one's own physical or mental attributes, that derive from arrogant pride.' While a narcissist closes all the doors around him taking pride in his self-worth, a person with self-love begins to open the same doors and be more loving towards others. While a narcissist may fail to develop a loving bond with others, a person with self-love will be motivated to spread the love within as well as outside of him. Loving yourself will make you feel at peace with yourself and once this feeling sinks in, there is no place for pride inside you. The inner bond will help you become calm, humble, grateful, emotionally stronger and at peace with yourself and that's when you will not repel your own company or prefer someone else's instead!

Another most common aspect which we all fight at some point is the 'fear of loneliness'. This fear clings to us like a life force and becomes one primary reason for keeping ourselves away from our own company. Most destructive relationships are born out of this fear. How? Here's an example:

In my internship years, I met a young girl, Sheena, who might have been around 22 years of age. She came to me for counselling to overcome her recent heartbreak. She had managed to date more than a dozen guys and had one steady serious relationship for 3 years. Her pattern was simple – she would get frustrated with one relationship, get out of it, and immediately, like the very next minute, jump into another one. Because she dreaded being alone and most of her friends had boyfriends, she accepted any guy who showed her little care and concern. This way, all her relationships would start with few rosy days and end with the crappiest days she ever witnessed. The longest relationship she was in, turned out to be the most abusive, and in spite of being unhappy with it, she refused to let it go. She said that she loved him and will wait forever to have him back. For her, that was love, even though the same love made her feel miserable every single day!

When I asked her about her need for constantly having someone by her side, even if that person made her feel like shit every day, she said she cannot be alone and that she hates to go partying when all her friends have boyfriends and she doesn't. So to cover up this gap, she would fit in anyone who came after one's exit and ensured that the space was never vacant.

When I met Sheena, I could totally relate to what she was feeling – the crave and need to have someone constantly love you every single day of your life; the desire to have someone who shows you unconditional love and support and who makes you feel like you are the most precious person on this earth. Gradually, when the initial affection starts fading, you, with the whole of your body and mind, begin to cling to that person. It becomes like an addiction, so much so that even if the drug you were taking starts damaging your whole being, you still crave for it and consider it to be vital for your survival. Knowing that the withdrawal symptoms are much worse and painful, you willingly agree to let go of everything that is in your control – your self-esteem, your pride, your priorities, your desires, your career, your happiness, absolutely anything that can get you the drug back.

So while I could connect to what Sheena felt and counseled her then, the actual first-hand experience happened when I underwent a relationship breakup myself. When my engagement with the so called 'love of my life' was called off, I was devastated. I had heard and read a lot about this whole 'self love' by then but nothing seemed to have worked at that very moment. While friends, family and relatives began coaxing me for another relationship (Marriage is the word!), something inside me told me to run away somewhere and take a break (in usual circumstances in the past, the same voice told me to find somebody else and get going). I was still craving for that addictive drug and did everything what Sheena did to get it back. The pain of not having that drug was unbearable.

In that state of ache and hurt, I reached a point where I couldn't bear my own company and I began craving for the drug (love) more. Thankfully I became a little occupied with fighting God (the 'why me' syndrome), crying and looking for ways to end my 'miserable' life, and thus succeeded in keeping myself away from the love-drug for a short time. This was possible because at some point, after years of struggle in knowing and valuing myself, I began to question if this is all worth it! If it is OK to continue clinging to one relationship after the other and be dazed and then die of this drug overuse one day! I decided to fight this and let myself go through the initial discomfort and fright of loneliness. Those were the toughest days of my life while I struggled to fight the loneliness out of my system. I desired to fill the empty space with someone (anybody for that matter!) every time I reached a point where the loneliness seemed unbearable. This is usually the time when we all give in to the temptation and begin to hop-skip-jump in and out of relationships. The innate urge of filling that gap with anybody takes over and we are even willing to walk around, sleep around with anyone just to fill that empty space within. Since I was in a fight back mode, I decided to fight it out alone.

I finally gave myself some time alone and the moment I did that, I unconsciously gave myself a chance to endure my own company. In the previous hop-skip-jump cycle, I never gave myself this time to think or be without someone else. The priority was always someone else! This cycle began to break when I gave myself five months of solitude. Those five months, I gave myself a chance to test my patience of being in my own company. It was tough! I am a very jovial person by nature, a complete extrovert and I never have difficulty building relationships, but this whole thing of building a relationship with myself was by far the most difficult thing that I did.

What I gained after those five months is something I can't even begin to describe. In those days, I learnt what is good for me, what makes me happy and gave myself all the love that I would have given to the person who filled that empty space in the past. I gave myself a chance to fill that vacant space within. I began to walk around alone and see places which I would have otherwise seen with a companion. I treated myself with my favourite food, started playing my favourite sport and entered parties all alone.

I kept telling myself, "It's OK, Shama. Don't be afraid of loneliness." I reminded myself of what Elizabeth Gilbert once said – "At some point, we all have to learn how to walk into a party or a restaurant alone. Otherwise, we will be willing to walk in with *anybody,* or worse, walk out with anybody. We have to learn how to endure our own company and hold our heads high. And sometimes, after enough time alone, we might even learn to enjoy ourselves." And I did exactly this – gave myself enough time to be with me, even though it began with frustration and left me feeling worse at times.

Finding happiness in your own company:

- The first step to this journey begins with knowing yourself (as mentioned previously). Once you start that process, write a note to yourself saying 'I love, embrace and accept myself just the way I am' and stick it at a place where you can see it every single day. Or the alternative is to keep reminding yourself of this by repeating it in your head, especially at times when your mind is on a self-critical mode. Remember, it is OK to be lonely. The need to have a companion is just your mind's intuitive reaction, scaring you with the feelings of uncertainty, anxiety, fear, loneliness and so on.
- Begin with giving yourself ten minutes every day. Get to know yourself better and do the things you love, all by yourself. Increase this 'Me Time' as the days pass by.
- Treat yourself like you are the most important person in your life. Engage yourself in various activities, starting with as simple as being alone while sipping tea/coffee (without phone or TV or music). Go out cycling, jogging, walking, trekking, exercising, cooking, painting, dancing, singing, weaving or do yoga to get in touch with yourself.

- If anyone comes to you showing pity (which many people would), listen to what they have to say and then remind yourself that the bond with yourself is much more important than the connection you establish with others. Example, when I go and sit alone at a coffee shop and I get call from my friends, they often wonder how I can sit by myself sipping coffee for hours. Their common response is - "What is wrong with you? How can you sit alone? You want me to come? Don't you get bored? Stop being a loner." I smile at myself and tell them very politely, "I am having fun and enjoying my company over a cup of coffee and my company is definitely not boring, don't you agree?" Sometimes I just don't give any justification at all!
- Write a thank you note to yourself each time you feel good in your own company.
- Write a letter to yourself at the time of crisis describing how you feel, just like you would tell a friend about the incident.

Today, I can hold my head high and walk alone anywhere in the world. I have come to understand what is good for me and this realization would prevent me from clinging to any relationship that brings me hurt and pain. This me-to-me connect makes me feel like the best person on this planet because I chose to make myself feel that way without anybody's support. And to arrive at this place, we all have to begin with saying, 'It is OK to be lonely'.

"I needed someone to pamper me,
love me unconditionally, spoil me and
never leave me. So, I married
Myself!"

3 Accept and Embrace Your Emotions

"The walls we build around us to keep out the sadness, also keep out the joy."

~ Jim Rohn

From the time we are born, we are subjected to gender bias in our society. We are expected to behave differently, based on whether we are male or female, in almost all aspects of life – mental, social, physical and emotional. While it is socially acceptable for a female to cry or be upset, it is considered as a sign of immaturity and weakness if a male does the same. While God created neutral emotions, the human brain conveniently went ahead and categorized them into masculine and feminine aspects of emotions. This categorization has been a part of our society since decades now. While we all have got it permanently tattooed into our system, very rarely do we pay attention to its hazards on our development and wellbeing. Though the trend has been changing in recent years and men are becoming more emotionally expressive, the genre continues to be gender bias, leading to more emotional complications.

As human beings, experience and expression comes naturally to us and the moment we try to curb it, it begins to cause internal damage without our conscious awareness. I had a 43 year old client who was brought in the Rehab for severe anger issues. His anger issues led to marital and family discord and he was left with fighting alone in Rehab with no loved one visiting to check on him. In the course of therapy while we were discussing his childhood, he started talking about his relationship with his mother. His father had passed away at a very young age and his mother forced him to get into family business whereas he wanted to purse his education in engineering. His mother feared that he might prefer a salaried job rather than taking care of his father's factory, so she refused to pay for his education, despite them being financially sound. He had to beg a priest of their church to fund his education. The mother-son conflict had a very harsh and lasting emotional effect on the client, but because he lived in a society where emotional expression (especially against parents) is considered taboo, he said he loved his mother throughout. He talked about how he was passionate about playing cricket and his mother would send him to sit at the factory instead. But he kept on insisting that he loves his mother very much and respects her for the values she instilled in him.

There were moments in the session where sharing of that past was so painful for him that he couldn't hold it all inside and let it out in the form of tears (Believe me! For a 43 year old male to cry in front of a younger female isn't easy at all). He cried sharing the anger he felt against his mother, for the playful childhood that was taken away from him, for every negative emotion and hurt he felt as a child and for all the responsibilities that were put on his shoulder at the age of fifteen.

Throughout his life, he had never shared this hatred or anger he felt as a child and neither was he ever appreciated for the responsibilities he fulfilled by not only going to the factory and taking the family business ahead but also by acquiring a degree in engineering with a first class result. All through his life till date, he kept holding that anger within him which only kept getting worse and eating him up within. While I could see the guilt of speaking against his mother visible on his face, I assured him that it was OK to express what he felt and it was time to let it go.

At the end of the session, he smiled and told me that it was first time in the last thirty years that he cried and it was the very first time that he spoke about his bitter childhood to someone. He was amazed to see that in the last sixty minutes that we spoke, not once did he feel angry or irritated. He confessed that he felt as if a big burden had been taken off from his heart and that he could breathe freely right now.

Often in our lives, when we experience hurt or pain caused by our loved ones, we remind ourselves that they have the right to do so. And we let that hurt float within us all the time. We refuse to talk about it because others might feel that we don't love our family or friends or don't respect them as much as we should! So we let it stay. Even when it starts eating us internally, we let it stay there safely. What we fail to understand is that it is OK to express the feelings, to let out the emotions that your mind and body is experiencing. While you are letting it out and even after you let it out, you continue to love the person with all your heart. Just by expressing how the person's act made you feel angry or caused you pain doesn't mean you are labeling the person as 'bad' or 'horrible'. It is not about the person. It is about your feelings caused by your relationship with that person. Often, the suppression of such emotions leads to complications which could have been avoided by simple expression of it.

In the above case, his anger would not have aggravated to a critical extent if he would have got the freedom to express what he felt and was assured that he was OK to be hurt and feel that hurt within. Because he was not allowed to experience or express weak emotions - hurt, pain, sadness, fear etc as a man, the only way out for him was to bottle up the sadness and hurt and channel it through the most available emotion i.e. 'anger'. So, while the process of acknowledging and accepting your emotions is healthier than you imagine, it is equally important to learn to express those emotions in a healthy way. When I say healthy, I mean physically, mentally and emotionally non-destructive.

While we all are attuned to the 'feelings' channel 24/7, we are rarely taught the art of tuning to the accurate frequency to get clear images. To put it in simple terms, while we do become capable of acknowledging and accepting the emotions, we struggle to let them out in a way that is less painful for us. To protect ourselves against uncomfortable thoughts, feelings, and experiences, we develop a set of automated mental reactions called defences, the psychological term for which is 'defence mechanisms'. We build these mechanisms suiting our needs right from childhood and continue to nourish it as a part of our personality all throughout. These defences act as protection (in our conscious mind) against painful feelings, thoughts or situations we experience in our lives. They not only filter out things we may not want to recognize but also change our perception to make the reality more comfortable and less painful. From a clinical perspective, it is a way of distorting the painful reality to arrive at a better conclusion that we can deal with.

While the use of these defences is very common and we all use it at some point or the other, it is more used by addicts to maintain addictive behaviours and thoughts (Note: one of the prime reasons for addiction is the lack of ability to acknowledge experience and express emotions). Some of the common defences[2] we use are denial, isolation, rationalization, blaming, etc. Using these mechanisms, we shut the door of emotions and its aftereffects and fool ourselves by saying that we have conquered it all! In reality, it is more damaging to our body, mind and spirit as emotions, to a large extent, control our thinking, behaviour and actions. Altering or falsifying emotions means damaging the other three areas of our being. What we think we have pushed back in our mind (repressed emotions) does not disappear in real time but gets deposited in our physical being in the form of body memories. In severe cases, these body memories result in physical illness, starting with something as basic as headache, stomach ache, leg pain, neck pain, shoulder pain and so on.

One of the theories of emotions practiced in ancient China documents that excess emotion causes damage to Qi (life force within each one of us; the spirit), which in turn, damages the vital organs. Thus, to avoid causing further damage to our being, it is required and almost necessary to ensure healthy experience and outlet of our emotions.

You may hear many people say, "Oh stop crying like a sissy. Grow up man! Fight it out" or they may advice you to always be shiny, cheery and perky and never experience the so-called negative emotions at all. From my practice and knowledge, I have come to believe that one should never let oneself fall for such foolish advice. It is common when I visit a funeral and see the family weeping and grieving for their loss, which is by far the most natural human instinct, and then are these people, sometimes the relatives who take charge or aunts and uncles of the community who think they are much wiser to handle such situations, constantly and continuously stopping the person from grieving.

There is a particular incident I remember where the girl lost her *bhabhi* during child birth with whom she was deeply attached. Her *bhabhi* left a new born son and a three year old girl behind with a husband who was more than devastated with the loss of the love of his life. So while she wanted to cry it out, and fight with God, asking why it had to happen to such a pure soul, there were these advisers asking her to stop crying and repeating words like, "If you cry, who will take care of your brother and family? If you don't stay strong, who will hold the family together? Come on, stop crying!"

While I do understand their concern, I am strictly against such gestures that don't allow someone to express freely what they feel. When we lose a loved one, we are in so much pain that nothing makes sense at that time. We don't want to see the logical side of things because we feel emotional about it. Crying and grieving during this time is the best form of self-healing. In the above case, imagine how miserable the girl would have felt after hearing that she has to be the strong one – she's already feeling emotionally crippled, and the guilt of not being able to hold the family together would have crippled her further and she would have concluded that crying or weeping is a sign of weakness, that she cannot afford to be weak because her family will be in pieces otherwise.

Emotions are meant to be experienced and expressed. It is OK to let it out - fear, hurt, pain, anger, whatever it is that you feel is bothering you. Don't sit and analyze the emotions. You have all the rights to experience every emotion inside you. Get in touch with it and release it – write it out, talk it out or therapy it out. The moment you get in touch with it, acknowledge it and begin to release it, you are automatically letting go of the negative energy within you, making more room for the positive one. Carrying this energy all around and making a grumpy face not only affects you as a person but also other people around you. A person who feels angry all the time is more likely to indulge in fights and snap at his family members or repel his colleagues at work. By simply discussing and talking about his anger, the person can contribute in making this world a happy place and not a crappy place.

While it is healthy to release your emotions, the world will be a good place if you also helped others release their emotions. When people come and talk to you about their loss or experience anger over some petty thing that happened at home, just be there to listen. Talking out is one of the best forms of emotional healing. Do not be judgmental or start giving them advice, even if you are most tempted to do so. Let them know that it is OK to feel what they are feeling at that moment, because feeling something isn't a choice we make. What we do after experiencing those feelings constitute our choices. Feeling something is innate, natural.

So the next time you experience a strong emotion, accept and embrace it, and avoid suppressing it. If you feel the world will laugh at you if you cry in front of someone, cry it out in a shower or write how miserable you feel about wanting to cry and not being able to do so openly.

Ways to accept and express your emotions:

- Write it out

  Writing is extremely cathartic. Write the incident that is causing emotional conflict and then write down the associated feelings. Write it to feel better and not with the intention of critiquing your writing style.

- Talk it out

  Look for a friend or any person with whom you can let out your emotional experience without being judged or criticized for the same. If you don't find such a person around you, look at your reflection and you will find at least one who's ready to listen to you without interruption.

- Engage in a physical activity

  Especially in the case of negative emotions such as anger or frustration, practicing a sport helps! Go out for a game or swimming or dancing or anything that involves physical workout (No, sex isn't included here). While you engage yourself in the activity, notice the bodily reactions and see if you can feel the negative unbearable energy exiting through each part of your body. Notice it, acknowledge it and if possible, come back and write about it - how you felt before the practice and how you feel after that. Embrace the emotion(s) as you begin to play it out.

- Ask for help

  Asking for help isn't a sign of weakness. No matter what you think, it is not about being vulnerable and dependable. By asking for help, you acknowledge the need to heal yourself which would make you only stronger and wiser with time. If you fall sick and it becomes unbearable for you to stay in that condition, what would you do? Go to a doctor and take medicines or stay home thinking that if you went to a doctor, he might call you a douche for not being able to take care of yourself? And once you do decide to take the medicine, do you feel weaker or does it actually make you feel better? Asking for help or visiting a counsellor is just the same. The difference here is not your physical health but your emotional wellbeing.

- Do not try to replace the emotions

  If you are feeling sad, it is wise to believe and accept that you are feeling sad. Admitting it is like telling your brain that 'green is green and green is not black.' Once you have experienced it and then if you wish to make yourself feel better, you can go ahead and listen to music or party or go for a movie. Curbing the hurt and pain immediately with alcohol or smoke or drugs is like feeding lasagna to a dying man who is on a ventilator. While the foreign material may have some feel-good effect on your brain, it is just another way of fooling yourself and seeing the world with rose-tinted glasses.

- The self-connect

  Stay connected with yourself. How? Remember the gut feeling that the world keeps talking about? Well, it's a result of this connect. Your body and mind will become more alert and help you protect yourself by giving you signs which you can identify only when you are in an emotional bond with yourself. Ever noticed that there are some people with whom we instantly click and feel safe in their presence while there are others from whom we get very discomforting vibes and we can't tolerate to stand in their presence for even a minute? If you haven't experienced this before, notice it the next time you interact with a stranger! These feelings are your mind and body's reaction to help you identify danger. Always, always trust this feeling, especially when you are encountering strangers. If your mind and body is filled with past emotional experiences and you don't vacate it, it may be too preoccupied then to help you gauge these signs. So un-clutter the clutter and make the journey towards an emotionally healthy 'You'.

4 Bursting the Bubble of Unrealistic Expectations

"God grant me the serenity to accept the people I cannot change, the courage to change the ONE I can, and the wisdom to know it's ME."

~ Anonymous

When I was born, I did not have a plan in mind as to how I would live my life for the next how many ever years I am alive. As a child, all I was interested in was playing and jumping around, and I couldn't make sense of why my family and other people around wanted me to behave in a certain manner. At every stage of my life, I had someone or the other to tell me how/why/what I should be ideally doing. When these faces and voices took a backseat, I realized that my own voice had then started giving me similar instructions. Each time I failed to listen to it or failed to fulfill it, a guilt feather would be added in my feelings hat. Right now, I probably have a dozen of these hats with guilt feathers arising out of just one word that began to unconsciously define my life, i.e. 'expectations'.

Now when I look back at my early years, I nod my head in agreement and say, "Ah! So this is where it all started. Right from the time I was born!" It took me most of my adolescent years to understand the term 'expectations'. The virus was introduced much before my poor brain could even comprehend it and as I grew old, it started becoming a part of each cell in my body. Everywhere I go or whoever I meet - strangers or acquaintances - they all seem to be affected by this virus. What's worse is that they start spreading it around as well, keeping it alive generation after generation.

The Oxford Dictionary defines the word 'expectation' as 'a strong belief that something will happen or be the case'. The explanation is purely futuristic and hence, by all means it is bound to create pressure on anyone who has a close encounter with it. We all have been a victim of this expectation virus at some point or the other, this term almost took the life away from us!

A 24 year old man walked in to the hospital at night complaining of severe chest pain. He collapsed ten minutes after he reached the casualty room. The nurses and doctor shifted him to the ICU while his friends remained dumbstruck as they heard the doctor say, "Cardiac arrest. Move fast." Two days later when he was shifted to the ward, I went to visit him to work on his psychological wellbeing. I still remember the expression he wore that day. He was shocked, scared, and petrified. He was instructed not to move around and was advised to stay in bed all the time. For a 24 year old to be dependent on someone can be a real nightmare, and this guy was actually living that nightmare. He relaxed a bit when I introduced myself as a psychologist and told him that he can talk to me about anything he wishes to, anything that's been playing on his mind. He began talking about how miserable he felt lying on the bed and unable to do as simple a task as getting up and reaching the nearest table to drink a glass of water. His eyes became moist as he started telling me more about his life and what led him to this hospital bed.

Arnab was a very bright young fellow. Right from a very young age, he was taught the art of 'excelling at everything' by his father. Very soon, it became a norm in his house to stand first in every exam. While Arnab did manage to excel in everything that he did, fulfilling his father's expectations soon became a necessity for him. He reached a point in life where he could not see himself not-excelling or not fulfilling his father's expectations. Not just academics, but also arts, extracurricular activities, sports, college union, social encounters, everything became a battle field for Arnab. He used to feel terrible when he stood 2nd or 3rd in several music and art competitions. He took it on himself that he has to conquer it all. The times that he failed to do so – like the time he stood second in class and got belted by his father because he missed the first position – he would beat himself to death saying what a useless creature he was on this earth.

Things worsened when he moved to another city to study engineering. The pressure of succeeding at everything became almost like a disease to him. He started developing frequent headaches as his anxiety level continued to increase by each day. The situation worsened when he fell sick during one of his exams and ended up failing in that particular subject. The pressure of letting his family know this was so severe that he put the entire blame on himself believing that he is a useless child. To curb his anxiety and bear the guilt of not meeting expectations, he started smoking and taking alcohol, although it began in small quantities.

While this went on for several days, Arnab confessed that there were times when he would feel choked and heavy in his chest. He experienced chest pain once or twice but concluded that it could have been due to acidity and he would conveniently consume Eno to ease the discomfort. The night he was brought to the hospital, he had suddenly developed the similar chest pain but this time it went beyond his ability to bear the pain, and he screamed out to his roommates who then rushed him to the nearest hospital. Arnab couldn't come to terms with the fact that he had a minor cardiac arrest at the age of 24. As he spoke to me, he mentioned how burdened he has felt and how heavy his whole body was with this load that he could not recognize within him.

Expectations can have that severe effect on each one of us. I have seen many people blame parents for giving birth to this virus, forgetting that the parents themselves may have been the victim of it as children and the time they had their children, the virus was already inside their mind, body and soul. The best example I can share here is of a paranoid father of a

2.5 year old girl who approached me and said, "My daughter just doesn't go to anyone. She howls and cries if someone even tries to come close to her. She's become very *ziddi*. Even at social gatherings, she becomes *ziddi* and refuses to behave well. All she has learnt is to cry and shout and we become embarrassed and fail to act as good parents in public."

Do you note here that the expectation isn't just from the child but even from 'self' too? I smiled at him and asked, "Do you remember you mother telling you how you were as a child?"

"I think I was a difficult child. I would run around everywhere and do everything that I was asked not to, I guess," he said.

"Well, that's what children at that age are supposed to do. They are not adults with developed social and moral rule books. They are meant to cry and howl and shout and scream because they don't have the ability to rationalize or critically examine their behaviour. When parents keep the child under their custody for two years without letting the child go to anybody and anywhere away from them, the child becomes accustomed to that touch and environment. That parental space is regarded as safe and happy. Now if you suddenly tell your girl to go shake hands with every stranger or go kiss and hug every aunt and uncle coming their way, she is bound to feel frustrated. And the only way children learn to find their way out is to cry loud. So while it comes naturally to you to expect your child to behave in a certain way, remember, she isn't an adult yet. Let her be a child. And you continue to be good parents as long as she loves to cuddle you, kiss you, throw tantrums at you and regards you as the place where she feels safe."

Most parents believe that it is healthy to have this pressure (either coming from them or coming from the child itself), as it is also capable of producing a positive competitive influence on the child's life and can motivate the child to do best. What they sometimes fail to understand is the demarcation between realistic expectations and unrealistic expectations. The line between the two is so thin and negligible that it doesn't take time to shift from the realistic to the unrealistic one. Once the unrealistic expectations make their base, they gradually start affecting the person's thoughts, behaviour and feelings.

Parents' expectations for their children often affect the children's perception about their own abilities. From childhood, these social or behavioural expectations often get internalized and become a strong belief pattern as we grow old. And when we become adults and arrive at a situation where our perception and belief isn't in alignment with that of our parent's, it results in internal chaos which sometimes becomes difficult to deal with. While parents are often regarded as a primary source of this virus, expectations and pressure do have other sources as well which can sometimes be greater than the parental influence.

To begin with, family becomes the first source, after parents of course, to list the do's and don'ts for the person – the ideal way to talk, behave, dress, succeed academically, become a famous person, acquire name and fame, pray, socialize and so on. The child is then exposed to school environment which becomes another source of developing pressure of expectations – academic success: 'good grades or else you won't get good job and people won't respect you if you don't have a good job'; if you fail to complete your assignments, you are labeled 'incapable of doing anything in life' and so on. Then at the same time are our peers, who continue to stay throughout our lives: you must be available for your friend all the time. If you aren't being available, you aren't being a good person. You must be loving, caring and supporting towards your friends even if that includes hurting yourself to make them happy. As you grow up and join the bigger rat race, your work becomes another influential source where the boss sets unrealistic targets that drains you mentally and physically, and yet it rarely reaches a satisfactory level. The society becomes another most profound source which gets connected to our lives through media, internet and people around who have the most perfect and ideal ways drawn for us on 'how to live a successful life'.

The next two points are my most favorite ones. I can talk for hours on these two sources of unrealistic expectations. These include romantic partners, combined with society and media influence.

So this person enters your life right at the time when your hormones and neural activity give up complete control on you. While experiencing love is the most amazing and powerful thing that happens to human beings (I promise I am not being sarcastic!), the relationship expectations which are set in front of us result in creating unbearable pressure on the human psyche. As a couple, before marriage, we wish to experience everything, every single emotion which is talked about in media and internet. Concepts like 'forever love', 'true love', 'the *janmo janmaantar ka pyaar*', 'the boy must fight for the love of his life', 'first love is the last love', etc become a realistic goal for us. I would take a risk here and say that this microbe is found in greater quantity in females. These concepts further distort the relationship when the couple decides to get married. You begin to hear phrases like - 'he changed after marriage' or 'she's become demanding after marriage' or 'this isn't the marriage I had imagined it would be' and so on.

What happens in such situations is that the unrealistic view of marriage or togetherness, the 'happily ever after' often shown in movies and TV and novels, is put face-to-face with the realistic side and the unrealistic world of the lovers begins to collapse right there! These unrealistic relationship expectations have been the cause of many suicidal cases and domestic violence – "I love him a lot. *Agar meri shadi hogi toh issi se hogi warna* I'll die. I can't stay without him anymore!" or "He is my *pati parmeshvar* and *bhagwan ka roop* so I should take anything and everything that comes from this *bhagwan*" or "I am married now. This is my life. I can't break it even if I'm not happy in it, because if I break it, I will put my family through a lot of shame and I can't let society point fingers at them for something that I am to be blamed for."

All these sources are combined in one single source and that is, 'You'.

By now, you have mentally, emotionally, physically and socially become capable of putting the most unrealistic expectations on yourself! The above voices become a part of you and you begin to live in the world of 'shoulds' and 'musts', grilling yourself to reach the place where the ideal 'you' belongs. You begin to remind yourself how important it is to meet the expectations of your peers, romantic partners and those demanded by work in order to feel a sense of belonging and approval. You begin to regard other's happiness as the only source of true happiness. You start over-pressurizing yourself at work to gain more money and status as that becomes an ideal way of acquiring everyone's respect and a luxuriously satisfactory life.

It is like racing towards an unrealistic life and self which is out there in the woods and you must get there in order to make sense of your existence. Stop.

Just take a pause. For a minute, bring your entire focus 'here'. Breathe.

For few more seconds, just know that you are

still breathing… at this moment, you have absolutely everything that is needed for your survival. Good, bad, OK, not OK, *you have it*. So for a minute, let yourself have what you already have and stop trying to have what you wish you had. The realistic life is who you are at this moment. The unrealistic perfect, almost non-existent life will only drain you physically, socially, mentally and emotionally. If not now, then at a later stage of your life, it will.

So while you continue to strive for the best, remember that it is OK to be the second best. It is OK to not meet expectations sometimes to protect yourself physically, mentally and emotionally. We all have a limit (a threshold) and I believe that it is healthy when we focus on strengthening the limit rather than exhausting it to a level where every cell of our body becomes compelled to give up.

How can you practice looking at yourself as a being free from expectations? To begin with, take a pause and acknowledge yourself – what you are, however you are. Practice this breather often during the day. Begin embracing yourself without trying to become the 'successful boss', 'the rich friend', 'the accomplished colleague', 'the perfect daily soap husband/wife', 'the ideal successful daughter/son' etc. You are all of it, but just in a different way. Because the virus is in every cell of our body, we continue to excel and compete with others in every aspect of life. It is time to de-condition that and begin to walk towards the realistic world where imperfection is not a flaw but a part of you that is waiting to be accepted, loved and cherished.

Remember

- Your physical, emotional and mental health is always a priority for healthy survival.
- The moment you feel you are beating yourself up to an extent that it aches - in the form of physical pain or emotional discomfort or increased substance intake - it's time to pause and stop.
- Note: The 'perfect you' exists in people's heads. Those people who themselves are an epitome of imperfection, and this character is purely *fictional.* You are perfect just the way you are, even if your brain and body refuse to accept this truth.
- It is OK if by refusing to fulfill someone's expectations, their sentiments are hurt. You need that in order to protect yourself from being stressed, pressurized or emotionally and physically hurt. Communicate your discomfort to them and if they continue to behave the same way, it is healthy to take charge and remind yourself not to give in to those painful unrealistic expectations.
- Every time you encounter an expectation, ask yourself if it is making you calmer, happier and giving you a breather to enjoy life without stress. If it isn't, open your eyes and see the red flag going up!

5 | *Failure is Inevitable*

"It is impossible to live without failing at something, unless you live so cautiously that you might as well not have lived at all, in which case you have failed by default."

~ J. K. Rowling

This 'F' word has been my companion from time immemorial. While it did give me a tough time, I came to believe that it will continue to exist in the world and pop up any time, at any stage, whenever it desires. So after 29 years of blaming, bitching, crying, hurting, we - failure and I - seem to have made peace with each other and understand each other's existence. It accompanied me all through my school years and kicked me on my face during my class 12 board exams. Failing an exam, in my opinion, was considered a hideous crime, and this one was just not any exam, but the boards. I failed in mathematics. I have come to learn that there are two things about you that every single soul becomes interested in knowing: 'What percentage did you get?' and 'When are you getting married?' Unfortunately, I have been the victim of both! So when I failed my boards in just one annoying subject, my world came crashing down.

When I came to know about my result, I was devastated. The immediate thought I had was not about how I would face myself, but how I would have to face the world! For me, it was more about how my family and friends would react and how the society - family friends, community people, parents' friends etc - would respond to this fatal incident. All this because I was so used to their feedback, criticisms and their idea of a 'perfect life' that I knew this incident would trigger a long list of 'How could she', 'Oh my God! She did? That's so shameful!', 'Her parents would have to go through a shameful time', 'Oh dear! Now who will marry her?', 'I knew she wasn't a bright child from the very beginning'. I can go on and on with this list. So while my primary goal could have been to take care of myself, pacify myself to ease the shock I experienced and deal with *my* failure, I added the guilt load on my back, focusing more on how others would see this failure. That whole perspective made me *believe* that failure is the most miserable thing you can let happen to yourself. It made me believe that I shouldn't and couldn't fail in life again, at any cost. If someone with this belief fails ever again, it literally becomes an end-of-the-world situation for them. Most suicides are committed for this sole reason.

With my red mark, I went into mental and emotional trauma. I stopped interacting with people, refused to go to any social gatherings, avoided calls and messages of friends who had passed, spoke bare minimum at home and worst of all, I lost 10 kilograms in two months. Every night, I religiously went through the cycle of 'Why me' questions to God, suicidal thoughts, endless crying and reaffirming my belief on what a wasted person I am. With this torture was another torture - studying for the supplementary math exam, especially since I hated math with every single cell in my body. So for a long time, I continued to believe I am a loser who *failed* and carried the guilt and shame all throughout.

It happens to most of us. The time of our life when we encounter failure, it becomes the most unbearable time of our life. And during that period, long or short, we fail to understand that it is momentary, that failure is a part of life and not the whole life. While it is almost impossible to understand this when you are experiencing the hurt/pain of failing, it is *required* to understand this once that phase has passed. How? Simply by telling yourself that it is a phase and it will pass. I practiced this too! I forced myself to walk past and look at other aspects of my life – my family was still with me, my friends still loved me and cared for me. And as days passed by, I gave my supplementary exam and enrolled myself for a certification course. A few more months and I was enrolled for a graduate course in Psychology and as I kept moving day after day, letting myself explore the chances at hand, I began to feel less burdened and realized that I was way ahead of that failure. I met people who weren't bothered about how much I scored in my exam as long as I was being good to them.

We all are immune to this constant fear of failure – failing at a job interview, failing in marriage, failing to become an ideal husband/wife/parent/daughter/son etc. People feel devastated when their relationship breaks. It's that vulnerable time when you can't stop figuring out why it happened and why it happened especially with you. Failure at this time usually becomes crucial to deal with! That's when we need to remind ourselves that it's not really the end of our world. This self-talk doesn't eradicate the failure or the sadness arising from it, but it does give you some strength to hold on as the time passes by. Bringing your focus to what is in your control - how to deal with failure - than focusing on what isn't/wasn't - the failure. This is one of the best things, and the healthiest way you can help yourself come out of the misery.

Take charge of making peace with this downfall. This 'taking charge' comes much easier once you begin to love yourself and value yourself, as that's when you realize that your feelings and your wellbeing are important and worth your attention.

The term failure is defined as 'the neglect or omission of *expected* or *required* action'. When you are expected to succeed or when you are required to succeed and if you happen to fail in those situations, the failure begins to eat you up from within. We all are pressurized every single day to *prove ourselves* as extraordinary human beings rather than just being one and shutting up about it. That's when we begin to exaggerate terms like success and failure and the after effects of both.

When I failed in 12th and when my engagement was called off, I let myself drown in a pool of self-pity and wondered why or how this could have happened to me. For ages, I had difficulty stopping myself from punching every face that told me, "Failure is good. It means you are being gifted with something bigger and better and good things are in store for you." And my response would be, "Really? You call this good? And good things are in store for me? Where the hell is that store then?"

Months after I had tasted the fruit of failure and while I was still trying to understand this whole 'failure is good' thing, I met an old friend over coffee. We got talking about life where I shared the story of my broken relationship and how I regarded that, and myself, as a big failure in my life. What she told me that day has stuck with me like a magnet and since then, I started feeling less pressurized with the whole success-failure saga. She had said, "OK. So you failed. That's sad. And that's fine. I failed too. Many a times! And I am still sitting here in front of you. Alive. So while I did get a feeling that failure will kill me, it didn't. It's OK to fail. Failure is painful but it doesn't kill people unless and until people *want* to kill themselves in the name of failure. So all you can do right now is believe that failure is unavoidable and inevitable. Sometimes you get chicken for dinner and sometimes you got to eat the *karela* because the butcher shops are closed. Crying over why the shops are closed or how could the shops be closed isn't going to help you open those shutters, and it also doesn't mean that the shops will remain closed for an eternity and you will never get to eat the chicken again. You are still healthy, alive and eating. It's a part of the deal called 'life'. And if you ask me why it is, well, we all have to do some more *mehnat* ourselves to understand why this life functions the way it does."

When she was done talking, I felt as if I was unnecessarily exaggerating this whole failure. I felt as if it really was not as big a deal as I'd made it out to be. That's when I looked back at the time when I failed in my mathematics exam in Class 12, and for the first time, I asked myself, "Why did I cry so much? I failed then but now I am a post graduate psychology student and a fine practicing counsellor!" I had never thought that I would go on to study masters after that failure, as I was convinced that I am not meant for anything that has to do with books and studies. I had refused to look beyond those results. What had seemed like an 'end of the world', then seemed like the silliest thing I ever did in my life. I find it silly today because now I refuse to define my worth based on the number of times I failed or succeeded. I define my worth based on how good the person within me feels in spite of having failed in life. I continue to stay alive even after I fail, so is failing really that big a deal in life?

"Success and failures are mental labels which become your sense of identity, your conceptual self," says Eckhart Tolle. The moment there is a threat to this conceptual identity, we begin to fall apart and our whole identity comes crashing down. Our whole life's meaning gets attached to these success-failure non-identical twins. And the definition of these non-identical twins is often exaggerated by the society, causing people more stress and forcing them to associate fear with both success and failure. So while failure and success continue to be inevitable, overcoming them is definitely in your control.

How can you overcome failure?

- Remind yourself every time, not just at the time of failure, that even though it may feel like the end of life, it isn't. You are feeling like that because your mind is conditioned to tell you that failure is bad. So even though you may feel like your world is falling apart, the world isn't collapsing for real.

- Feel sorry or sad for it. It is OK to cry over failure. I personally feel it's therapeutic, but when you do feel sorry, make an effort to step out of this emotional self-pity zone and focus on the areas of your life which you are grateful for! Example, you may have lost your lover but you have a perfectly healthy body, you still have a family and your friends, your education, job, house etc. And even if everything or everyone goes away, you still have the gift of life with you.
- Make a list of all your good times, your success stories and your most memorable moments. The next time failure hits and you feel all crappy about yourself and life, pick up those stories and remind yourself that there's more to life than one failure.
- Acknowledge other areas of your life where you haven't failed. If you fail to become an extraordinary student, you may still have succeeded in becoming an extraordinary friend or a lover or a daughter or just a humble loving human being. List as many areas as you can and then see the whole life wheel in totality. The failure would then feel miniscule, even though you may continue to feel sad about it.
- Elizabeth Gilbert's 'Jar of Happiness': Every night, write down one happiest moment of your day, fold the chit and put it in a jar. Let the jar collect all your happy moments and open it up and read them when you begin to feel that your whole world has turned upside down.
- Know that mistakes are going to happen and you have a right to be imperfect. This imperfect 'you' is a part of the 'perfect you', so embrace it with love and care.

6 | Self-pity? Get Over It!

"Self pity is easily the most destructive of the non-pharmaceutical narcotics; it is addictive, gives momentary pleasure and separates the victim from reality."

~ John Gardner

"I don't deserve this. She treats me like shit! I don't know why it always happens with me. Life is really unfair to me all the time," said one of my clients, a 23 year old man. Throughout the course of therapy, he wore a 'poor me' mask and never failed to narrate how life has had only struggles for him and how he had to face hardships right from childhood. What seemed like a casual ranting and venting out for first two sessions, became a pattern for acquiring emotional attention. In such situations, even if you try to bring the focus of the person on the things that aren't screwed up in their life, they refuse to look at this side of the existing reality. For them, they feel safe, comfortable and secured in this 'self-pity' mode.

We all wear this mask at some point or the other. The problem arises when this behaviour becomes a habit. While it seems like they are seeking help as they are venting out, most times it is just to get the sympathy of others and nurture their 'poor me' energy around. People who bask in self-pity love to play the victim and unconsciously believe that they cannot do anything to turn the course of their life. They usually develop a tendency of depending on someone else to rescue them from any given situation. People who have this self-pity mode turned on all the time develop a pattern of continuously seeking an external validation for their poor self. For instance, if a wife with a habit of basking in self-pity finds out that her husband has developed a chronic disease, she would bring the attention to herself, highlighting how difficult it is for her to stay in this situation, rather than talk about the husband's disease and how it is difficult for him to survive it. She would focus more on how this problem has made her life the most difficult one! People who develop this tendency often begin to look for problems around them and find solace when they discover a pity situation for themselves.

I had a friend in college who loved to narrate the struggles and problems of her life. She would not only talk about it to her close friends, but to anyone who would express the willingness to spend some time with her. While she did go through some tough times in her life, having lived in a broken family where her parents did not get along and her alcoholic father had an extra-marital affair with another married lady, the 'continuous talking about it' became annoying at times. So while I did feel sympathetic and empathetic towards her and would often offer her a shoulder to cry and crib, it started becoming difficult to even be in her presence. She would crib every single day about how some or the other part of her life isn't fine. Her friends showed her the good side of her life, but she would return back to the difficult side and stay there forever. She refused to acknowledge the possibility of being able to stay happy even if her life seemed twisted and broken in the past.

The company of such people usually creates a very negative energy around and you feel completely drained when you spend few hours with them. Wikipedia defines the term 'self-pity' as 'the psychological state of mind of an individual in perceived adverse situations who has not accepted the situation, and has neither the confidence, nor competence, to cope with it. It is characterized by a person's belief that he or she is the victim of unfortunate circumstances or events and is therefore deserving of condolence.'

From the time we are born, we get used to

receiving attention from others. In the first few years, we are made to believe, though words, gestures and actions, that we are the most precious thing existing on this planet. If we fall and get hurt, the whole world seems to come by our side to check if we are OK. So when someone who's attuned to such attention grows up, he/she often exhibits this attention-seeking behaviour and unconsciously starts enjoying it.

Each time we get hurt, we go on the auto-pilot mode of feeling and feeding this 'poor me' monster. While some of us may begin to unlearn this pattern, many people begin to seek this pity unconsciously. Such people lack self-esteem and often end up being alone, complaining that the other person - a friend, romantic partner, siblings, best friends etc - has betrayed them in relationships. They will sit and cry about how the other person treated them or used them and then may attract another similar relationship through empathy, repeating the same cycle all over again.

To be able to enjoy life to the fullest and have a positive approach to life, the self-pity block should most definitely be removed. Life is miserable sometimes and we all love to feed on undue love and care in those times, but making that a habit will only create a belief that 'happiness, love and comfort always comes from an external source'. To break this cycle, it is necessary to start feeling rich inside. The more rich and fulfilled you feel from within, the more you will be able to stay away from drowning in the poor-me sea.

All these people seem to have got it all sorted and I have no idea what's going on with my life!

The first step to get out of the self-pity pool is to remind yourself that winning isn't going to resolve anything. If you notice a pattern in you, perhaps you have a habit that you unconsciously begin to talk about the miseries of your life, remind yourself that you are not the only person with problems and having a problem is a sign that you *need to* look for a solution and not sit and relish the problem. If need be, kick your own ass or ask a friend to do so and shake yourself up each time you feel the melancholic blanket being wrapped around you. If you have a friend who you think bathes a lot in the self-pity pool, confront them about this habit. Tell them how this behaviour affects your relationship and how it will be worth if they stopped feeding on emotional drama created by their own selves.

When you find yourself in this mode, remind yourself that you deserve to live a happy life and you are capable of doing the same. Receiving sympathy from others may make you feel good but in the long run, that attitude will only distance you from your loved ones. Create a gratitude section on your notice board and keep pinning every small or big thing or instances that made you feel good about life. Place this gratitude board where you get to see it every minute of every day. This board becomes a reminder for you that life can also be good, and that life *has* been good.

How can you be less self-piteous?

Replace the sentences on the left whenever you feel them forming in your head with more positive ones, as indicated on the right:

Self-piteous phrases	*Positive statements*
Life is unfair to *me.*	Life is unfair to *everyone* but life is also fair at the same time.
I feel used and cheated by her/him.	Even though I feel used and cheated, it is solely in my hand to stop feeling used and cheated. I *can make myself* feel valued and loved.
I can't help it.	*Only I can* help it. I *can* unwrap the melancholy blanket if, and whenever I wish to.
I wonder how and why it happened to me.	It *has* happened (past). What is happening *right now* can be a new creation. It does not have to be governed by my past. I am willing to embrace my present and let go of my past.
I feel so miserable.	I approve and value myself.
Nobody loves me, nobody cares for me.	I love and accept myself the way I am and I will let go of self-pity. I am surrounded by people love me and care for me.

Just like you are capable of drawing others' and your own attention to problems, you are equally capable of drawing that same attention to the non-problematic areas of life. Even if there are problems in life, coming out of them and sailing through them to reach another end is an ideal process. The moment you kick yourself to get out of the self-pity pool, you will begin to stop hating and start loving your life.

Note: It will be a tricky process because your mind may continue to lead you to the self-pity path each time you try to walk away from it. In these situations, filling the gratitude wall and practicing the affirmations will help de-condition the monstrous mind.

7 The Blame Game Futility

"The blame game is already a lost game, so don't attempt dressing up to play it! Blames create no change; winners don't apportion blames!"

~ Israelmore Ayivor

We all are in a process of creating something new every single second of our life, through our thoughts, behaviour or action. This creation not only affects us as individuals, but also the people around us. Thus, whatever the current state of world, we are equally responsible for it. Given this phenomenon, there are many 'ego saints' who refuse to even look at this phenomenon. For them, life and the world work on only one principle - "I am OK, you are *not* OK"[3]. This is a vicious, additive game that we all love to play often in our lives – The Blame Game.

Ever seen a small child fall down while running, walking or playing? If he/she falls flat on the floor, the mother or other family members rush there, hug the child and start hitting the floor saying, "*Aww mera bacchha gir gaya*? *Maaru iss floor ko*? Floor is very bad, you hurt my baby… hit, hit…" Similar things happen when a child hits the table or bumps into anything. It is always the table's fault. The concluding lesson the child learns here is - 'it is always someone else's fault and not mine. Simple! There it is! You taught me this so I am going to practice it all my life. It makes my life much simple and easier.' So right from an early age, the ego learns to find fault in others and if someone reminds the ego that the fault is its own, it quickly puts on rose coloured glasses to avoid looking at the reality.

So while we all have been playing the blame game since time immemorial, it becomes a concern when playing this game becomes a habit. The person starts blaming the external forces for their internal state of wellbeing. The best example of this is found in marriages where couples excel in playing this tug-of-faults game. I once had a client who blamed his wife and his marriage for every single thing – His car broke down, the wife would be at fault; The boss is an ass, the marriage is at fault, since he couldn't give more quality time to work because of it; He's put on 7 kgs in the last 5 months, the wife is at fault; He gets late to office, the wife is at fault because she didn't wake him up on time and delayed the breakfast and so on…

My Blame Board

Who do you blame whenever something makes you unhappy? Tick mark options in the following list and review your feelings when it comes to blaming others. You're free to add more options.

- Graha/stars/horoscope
- Destiny
- Time

- God
- Karma
- Society
- Neighbours
- Government
- Upbringing
- Family/parents
- Boss/colleagues
- Friends
- Teachers/education
- Husbands/wives/GFs/BFs
- ____________________
- ____________________
- ____________________
- ____________________
- ____________________

While we get busy finding faults in others, our life begins to take a step back each time it happens. Though we continue to move ahead in time, our growth gets stunted. We refrain from taking responsibility of what we feel, what we believe, our behaviour, actions and experiences. We place our ego at a pedestal and each time it feels slightly threatened, it throws back the blame ball in someone else's court to ease the anxiety. Sometimes, even the realization that it could be your fault or you are responsible for your situation creates uneasiness, which the ego finds it difficult to deal with. Remember the character Silencer from 3 Idiots? He would always fart and say, "I didn't do it... Raju?" That's what we do, "I didn't do it... Destiny?"

We are taught how we can blame others, but never given lessons on how to deal with the anxiety that arises from accepting our fault, taking charge or being responsible for our actions. We get trained in blaming our stars, destiny, *samay*, the red light at the signal, the rains and every possible thing that exists around us. It eases the immediate anxiety and creates an illusionary world and belief that someone else is in charge of our life and for what happens to us.

Since we all have practiced this game for years together, it becomes a little tricky to unlearn it in a day. It is good to begin by taking baby steps in unlearning that behaviour which often makes you distant from your loved ones. The first step to do so is to remind yourself that you, and only you, are responsible for what happens to you in your life.

Each time you notice that you are pointing a finger at someone else, pause right there! The point here is not to find out who's at fault, but to figure out what you can do to make the situation better. So even if your mind tells you that your neighbor's dog was responsible for making you late, ask your mind to focus its valuable time and energy on what can be done now that you are already late. Blaming others for a situation and not focusing on how to make it better is like standing in a mud puddle and cursing the mud for making your feet dirty rather than walking out of it. When some people identify this behaviour or accept that they need to change, they often complicate it further by inventing a new game called Self-Blame, which also leads to self-pity.

There is a difference between self-blame and self-accountability. My all-time favorite author Elizabeth Gilbert explains this phenomenon beautifully. "It's a tricky metric, because self-accountability can sometimes be confused with self-blame. And I don't know any happy people who practice dreadful self-blame. Because self-accountability does not mean saying, "I fucked up, and I'm the worst person who ever lived." Nope, self-accountability means saying, "Well, that didn't go the way I expected it to, or wanted it to. But now I will put in the effort to learn from that experience and to grow."

Many people can help you grow in life but only you can nurture yourself by owning what happens to you and your life. The next time you think someone else is at fault, stop and ask yourself, 'what is in my control?' and then act according to it. Do what is in your hand to make the situation better. The fairies and genies come to save you only in the fictitious world. In the factual world, you become your own genie, your own guardian angel. Each time you begin to blame the external factors, bring your focus and attention to the inside. You are creating your life; others aren't creating or shaping it on your behalf. Since the creation is in your hand, the alteration is also a part of your nature. If your being starts feeling anxious, remind yourself that it is OK to make mistakes and it is fine to learn from your experiences. You don't become a useless person or a turkey if you take charge of your life when it seems messy or bumpy.

Start using your own wings and stop borrowing wings from others and then cribbing about how fragile, weak and defected they are. Take charge for a simplified life. Take charge for a better life. Take charge for a happy life. Remember, you are breathing for yourself and only you can breathe for yourself.

Activity: Board – 'I Am' My Own Genie

List down what 'YOU' can do to make your life better/ happy/peaceful/worth living. Each time you feel an excuse creeping up, immediately look for a solution before the list of excuses increase. Excuses are just your ego's way of telling you that it is not in your control. Remind yourself that you are responsible and capable of your own creation and then work your way out of the blame game or self-pity trap.

8 Accepting Help Will Not Belittle You

"Be strong enough to stand alone, smart enough to know when you need help, and brave enough to ask for it."

~ Ziad K. Abdelnour

'Seeking help' has been associated with inability or weakness from the very existence of human race. A person who asks for help is often considered to be inadequate, imperfect and incapable of taking care of his own life. We are often taught to embrace struggles and miseries on our own but never to ask for help because that may weaken us further. Please note here that asking for help in your struggle doesn't make you weak but struggling to fight it alone, does!

I had a friend who would hesitate a lot in coming to me for help. And whenever she did, she would feel so indebted and burdened that she would wait for a chance to repay - in action - the help that was offered. When I saw this pattern in her, I assured her that asking for help isn't a crime or a legal bondage that you must help your helper. A helper often offers help because he/she genuinely wants to help without any favors in return. Look at it this way - If someone you know was suffering (physically, mentally or emotionally), wouldn't you offer your support to them? If someone you know is going through a difficult situation, wouldn't you offer help to them? In fact, you may expect them to come to you in such situations and feel good about it when they approach you. Sometimes this even strengthens the bond between people.

Seeking help isn't the same as running away from your problems or dumping the problem on someone else. Some people get habitual of asking for help for trivial things and keep asking someone else to fix their life. This isn't healthy and this behaviour will only take you further away from your loved ones. Asking for help is a process where you seek support but at the same time, you continue to take charge of your life in executing that help. It is about getting help once so that the next time you come across the same situation, you learn to manage it on your own. In any tough situation, it is healthy to try and fix yourself first and only when you feel you need a helping hand to cross the bridge, you ask for help.

People often feel burdened, guilty, fearful and uncomfortable while seeking help. This is probably because we are taught that 'it should always be give and take'. That is why, at any given moment when we receive any help, our mind alerts us that we have become indebted to give, even if the person doesn't need help from us. It usually happens in friendship – a friend who seeks emotional support from the other often wonders why the other person isn't coming to her for the same. Some people even say, "I share everything with you. I even take your help when I have any problem but you never come to me. You never take my suggestion or advice. We are friends *na*! You know you can count on me, right?" We all need someone or the other at some point in our lives, especially when we feel we've reached a dead end, so know that:

a. You don't become indebted to the helper in a way that you *must* help them immediately. If they need help from you, they will come to you.

b. It is OK to seek help.

c. Seek help, but take charge of fixing your own life.

When you encounter emotional struggle in your life, it is vital that you de-clutter the internal mess. If you feel that no one around is able to help you feel better, seeking professional help - counselling - is the best thing you can do to protect yourself from getting emotionally drained. Seeking help for your emotional difficulties will only help you get stronger and bring clarity in your thought process.

Easy ways to seek help

For those of you who find it difficult to ask for help, here are some ways to make it easy:

- Accept that you need help and keep your ego aside

  Some people wait for the 'help' to walk up to them. Even though they feel the need of getting help, their ego bar is at its peak, which forces them to deny the need for assistance. My grandmother was so determined on staying independent that at the age of 90 when she had to climb the stairs, she would refuse to take any hand offered to her, preferring to take support from the railing or other stairs. I was proud of her independent nature, but I often saw traces of ego stopping her to seek any help from others. The ego will always continue to stick around, so make a habit of dropping it down every now and then, especially when you need help. Standing in front of a closed door and refusing to ring the doorbell will only make things difficult for you.

- List down the problem areas and people who can help you in it

  At a de-addiction center, many alcoholics and addicts are made to practice the power of seeking help. Addicts and alcoholics usually find it very difficult to accept that they need help. They are made to repeat and re-affirm that they need help and are asked to make a list of people who they can approach at the time of crisis. So in the postrecovery phase when they feel the craving for the drug, they remember who to call immediately and seek help. Make your own list of problem areas and identify people who you can approach for help. This will be your step towards easing the complications in your life.

- Express gratitude

  If you want to actually see gratitude in its purest form, meet a person in need who has been offered help. Their expressions and love would give you an exact definition of gratitude. Expressing gratitude makes you more humble and creates a positive feeling within you. It's a form of blessing exchanged between the helper and needy. However small the help may seem, feeling grateful is a sure shot way to happiness. If you think you haven't expressed gratitude to people who may have helped you in the past, do it right now and see how that makes you feel. Call them, leave a 'thank you' note or a message, visit them with flowers or show any other gesture. It doesn't matter what it is as long as the expression is straight from your heart. Always continue to wear the 'Gratitude Hat' and you will never experience problems with your ego.

Remember:

- Each one of us, as human beings, needs help.
- Not everyone will be willing to help you. So if you get a 'no' from one person, look for another. Remember it's your need and not the other

person's.

- When someone refuses to help you, don't waste your time by sitting and feeding your ego. The helper is free to choose whether to offer help or not.
- Most helpers may continue to remind you all your life that they helped you. Stay calm. It's a defect they have, so don't take it personally. Each time they remind you, smile and say 'yes you did. And I am grateful to you for it'.
- Some people may act like they are helping for numerous reasons – they may be finding it difficult to say no to you or they may not want to help you for pure selfish reasons. It is OK. Remember, they are free to make a choice. So the moment you learn the truth, step aside and knock another door. Pumping your ego in such situations and throwing tantrums like, "how dare he!" or "I will teach him a lesson for this" will only worsen your state of mind.

Activity

List down names of your best potential helpers, for different situations:

____

____

____

____

____

OK! SO,
you need help
I need help
In being able
to ask for
help.

9 | Be a Miracle For Someone Else

"Before death takes away what you are given, give away what there is to give."

~Rumi

"I think offering help to others is euphoric in itself. You do it because it comes from within and the key is to overcome the expectation of getting something in return. You help because it makes you feel good. I like to help people – be it my known friends or strangers, because I know that they have a need which I don't. If I can fulfill that need for them, then why not? It makes me happy. And makes them happy too." These words were said to a documentary film-maker by an elderly lady. Helping others is the quickest and easiest way to experience happiness.

If you wish to know how you can experience it too, try this:

- Be observant of your surroundings, wherever you are: Your locality, the metro, park, mall, work, home, etc.
- If you spot a person struggling with something,

maybe as simple as lifting a heavy bag, smile at them and ask, "Do you need help?"

- If they say yes, go ahead and help them.
- Pause to notice the genuineness in their expression when they express gratitude. Try it with the elderly, labor class or poor people.
- Feel that liberating feeling within and be grateful for your ability to offer help, for it could be you on the other side of the line in the near future!

Offering help to others without expecting any favors in return is little tricky, but the more you practice it, the more it becomes easier. In my profession, it often becomes challenging for me to curb my urge of helping someone in need. We all love to offer help at some point and the *josh* of helping gets so high that we feel irritated if the other person refuses to ask or accept our help. When I see people struggling with emotional issues and I can see that counselling will help them, it becomes challenging for me to hold myself.

When it comes to helping others, it is important to note that you can only make the person aware that help is close to them. To seek it or to receive it is their choice. They are free to say yes or no to your gesture, so don't be heartbroken and sad or call the other person a fool. Just how you have a choice to offer or not to offer your help, the person is free to make a choice too.

We all wish to see this world becoming a better place to live-in and the easiest way to make that happen is to practice one good deed every day. Make an effort to offer help wherever possible – be open to offering and receiving help. This way, your ego will take a back seat and humility will start ruling your mind and heart. Think of the last time you helped someone and remember how you felt at that time! Did you give a car ride to your colleague when it was quite late for public transport? Did you buy a pack of cookies from a street kid even when you did not need it? If you wish to continue feeling liberated like that every day, be more open to giving.

Remember:

- Many people may not express gratitude or be thankful for your help. It is OK. They have a choice just like you do.
- Helping is not to be limited to hot or sexy chicks or handsome men. It is universal.
- The hot receiver may say a 'no' to your help, and that doesn't mean that you are an incapable, useless douche. There is also a line between wanting to help someone genuinely and helping just to impress someone. Learn to draw that line.
- Helping someone to gain something in return isn't called helping. That process is called 'using' or sometimes 'abusing'. Be aware to know the difference between the two when you are at the receiving end.
- We love fixing other's lives but remember, while you may offer help in fixing, you are neither capable nor responsible for fixing others life (husbands and wife make a special note of this

point for each other's happiness).

If you offer help to the best of your capacity and the problem still persists, don't take it all on yourself. You can help the person fix things but you cannot fix it all for them. For e.g. a doctor may try his best to save a patient's life, but if still the patient doesn't get better and passes away, it doesn't mean the doctor did not help him/her to the fullest. He did everything he could in his capacity. A similar example is when you help a depressed friend, but he/she still fails to stay upbeat about life. You cannot blame yourself because you could offer what was in your capacity and the friend needs professional help.

"Your hand opens and closes, opens and closes. If it were always a fist or always stretched open, you would be paralysed. Your deepest presence is in every small contracting and expanding, the two as beautifully balanced and coordinated as birds' wings." — Rumi, *The Essential Rumi*

So remember to give (when needed) and receive (when needed) and be grateful for the two!

10 | Stay Connected

"We cannot live only for ourselves. A thousand fibers connect us with our fellow men; and among those fibers, as sympathetic threads, our actions run as causes, and they come back to us as effects."

~ Herman Melville

Most people have a tendency to isolate themselves at the time of emotional crisis. We fear that we may not be understood by others or may be labeled as cranky, depressed or weak. Since man is a social being by nature, staying in touch with others is an innate human need. When we begin to refrain from this need, we begin to create a void within ourselves that leads to further discomfort and loneliness. The need for love, care and acceptance is usually fulfilled when we stay connected with our loved ones. In cases where people stay away from family, for study or work, it is important to keep that familial bond alive even while you are physically away from them.

There may be times where we might feel that we are not being understood by our family and conclude that they don't care about us, but remember that one, or even fifty such situations, cannot cut the tie of the familial bond we share with them. I once counseled a 15 year old girl who had major emotional issues with her mother. Her father had committed suicide and the mother re-married, leaving the children with their maternal grandmother. The girl had been holding a grudge against her mother for five long years because she had not wanted her mother to re-marry. The mother made every effort to make amends and explain her reasons for taking that step, but the girl refused to listen and continued hating her. In one of the sessions, I made her do a role reversal. It is a technique used in counselling where the client is made to play the role of the other person - the one they have a conflict with, and the counsellor plays the role of the client. Then the same troubled situation is acted out. At the end of that session, the girl cried her heart out when she began to see the whole situation form her mother's point. Usually in such techniques, when the client wears the other person's hat, he/she ends up taking similar steps or decisions in the role-play that the other person must have taken in reality. If not that, they tend to have a clarity of the whole situation and begin to understand why something happened the way it did. The girl couldn't believe how she had been so cold-hearted when her mother tried to do all of that just to protect her children.

As children, it is good to remind ourselves that our parents or grandparents have their personality, behaviour and values shaped by the upbringing they encountered, which is very different from ours. To change your values, beliefs and culture with time and becoming modernized doesn't come easy. It is like someone asking you to stop wearing jeans and start wearing *salwar* suits or saris every day. Would you accept this change? You might laugh at it but never change your whole being around it. So imagine how tough it would be for our senior family members to change and accept something they haven't ever practiced. The transition isn't as easy as it appears, so give them some time. It is not about who's right or wrong, or who needs to change, but it is definitely about understanding the perspectives and respecting those to strengthen the emotional bridge.

While we all still continue to have minor/ major conflicts with our family members, friends or romantic partners, it is important to work on sorting the relationship rather than disconnecting ourselves from it, unless it is some physical, emotional or mental threat to your life, in which case, it is best to seek professional help. Disconnecting may seem like an easy step but in the long run, we tend to develop that as a habit, and then each time we encounter a relationship tiff, we disconnect (the flight syndrome). This only brings us more isolation and a repeated pattern of cutting ties with people around.

Staying connected with your loved ones is a key to living a happy and balanced life. It is OK to run away from everyone - mentally, emotionally or sometimes even physically - to sort things out in your head but once you feel that you have collected your broken pieces together, get back to your home. Get back in the vicinity of your loved ones. If someone continues to hurt you, you are indeed free to take a step back and let them exit from your life, but breaking ties with all others is a clear invitation for loneliness and depression. At any time of crisis, this connect will make you feel loved. This connect will make you hopeful that you aren't alone in this world and that there are people who care for you, and your survival matters to them.

Visit your friends and family at least once a week.

You have to make conscious efforts to take time out from your mechanical work-life. Call them not just at the time of need but even on regular days where everything seems hunky dory. Express your gratitude to them whenever you can. Sustain that human touch and use it as a weapon when unhappiness and loneliness dares to come closer. Socialize whenever needed and socialize especially when you feel that you are going into the self-pity mode.

Socializing is often powerful because as human beings, we are constantly exchanging energies. Sometimes you may have noticed that you enter a place or meet someone and you suddenly begin to feel powerful, lively or positive from inside. Staying in the company of such people lifts your positivity and crushes the negativity out of your system. Hence, instead of sitting at home and feeding that negative energy, it is best to step out, connect with people and let their positive energy uplift your spirit. Many people hit the bar in such situations and bar is a place where negative energy can be easily exchanged, so it is more likely that you may end up attracting someone else's negative aura and bring it back with you, feeling all the more emotionally and neurologically wasted.

Staying connected doesn't mean bonding only in the virtual world – Facebook, Twitter, Gtalk, WhatsApp, Viber etc. Connect with others on a personal level by making efforts to meet them. Being in touch with your loved ones always creates a niche of happiness and if you wish to stay close to love, care and happiness, stay connected with your near and dear ones.

11 Accept and Embrace Individual Differences

"Christian, Jew, Muslim, Shaman, Zoroastrian, stone, ground, mountain, river, each has a secret way of being with the mystery, unique and not to be judged"

~ Rumi

Imagine a world where everyone you come across is a mirror image of yourself - the way they talk, behave, react or feel, their manners, values and beliefs are a replica of yours. In this world, you can then easily get to know what the other person is thinking or feeling because your copies exist everywhere. Would you be happy in such a fictitious world or would you then wish for things to be different?

I am glad and grateful that things are different in this world – not 'good and bad' or 'right and wrong' or 'superior and inferior' – just *different*. These differences exist in almost everything - nature, humans, animals, man-made things - ever since this world was created. While some of us prefer winters, there are others who love monsoon; while some love moonlight, others like sunshine; while some adore beaches, the others prefer to hike through mountains. When we choose one of the two, it does not make the other one inferior or bad or wrong. It is simply different and most of us respect and accept these differences in nature. We don't say, "Oh look! The moon is so beautiful. Why can't the sun be white and gorgeous like the moon?" However, when it comes to human differences, we often fail to respect and accept those differences.

Intellectually, we all know that every human being is different from the other. There can be few similarities in physical features or behaviour or thought process, but every person you meet continues to be different in various aspects. It becomes easier to accept the similarities but somehow, we all consciously or unconsciously begin to take charge of changing people around because we fail to accept and embrace the part of them that makes them different from the rest. We start labeling their actions, personality, behaviour, thoughts as good/bad or right/wrong simply because it does not match with the ideal human image we have established in our heads.

That's when, especially in relationships, we gradually begin to customize people, our partners, friends, family, to suit our needs. It is then that we begin to make comparisons between people. 'Her husband is so supportive at home, why can't you be like him?'; 'His parents allow him to party and spend money on anything he wants. Why can't my parents be the same?' These habitual conditions often give rise to irritation, anger, frustration and make it difficult for us to survive with someone who isn't a mirror image of ourselves. It is important to understand that our parents or elders behave in a certain way according to the values, behavior they have learnt while growing up. If your parents learnt and experienced that education is the most important thing in this world, it is most likely that they will teach the same to you and give importance to education over everything else. So, sometimes it helps to see where your elders are coming from, in terms of values and beliefs, to understand their perspective which may be different from yours. This helps in embracing the differences and respecting it rather than getting annoyed by it and labeling the other person wrong. Next time you come across a difference of opinion in your partner, try to understand why they feel the way they do, what is their perspective, rather than forcing them to accept your understanding of truth and righteousness.

Accepting and embracing differences in people is a key not just for own happiness, but also for happier relationships. One of my clients once said, "My husband just doesn't express! I get upset and angry and let it all out on him, but he never expresses his emotions. Sometimes I feel he's just not there for me when I need emotional support. He starts giving solutions to problems when all I want him to do is just sit and listen to my ranting without telling me what to do about it!"

It is a well-known idea that men/husbands are not wired to deal with emotions the way females are (exceptions excluded). If you want someone to listen to your ranting, it's best to do that with a female best friend. Men are conditioned to be more logical in nature and hence, each time they listen to a complaint or problem, they start looking for solutions. In a romantic relationship, we often expect our boyfriend or husband to be our best friend and when they fail to be both, we come across statements like – "He just doesn't get that I am upset" or "How can he not see I am hurt and pissed off?" Well, men don't usually understand the silent language or un-communicated words and that is what makes them different from women. Likewise, there are many features[4] that make 'him' different from 'her', and understanding and accepting this is a simple key to happy living.

No man understands the woman, no woman understands the man, and that is the beauty of their being together. - Osho

You are different from everyone else. You are not supposed to fit the 'perfect life partner' definition that your lover has created in his/her mind, neither can you have a person who can act, think, feel, behave just the way you deem perfect. Because we are conditioned to live in a society that offers different treatment to each one of us at every developmental stage, our personalities are bound to be different. The rules of 'good/bad', 'right/wrong', 'superior/inferior' were created by people for social convenience and since we have been taught these rules for decades now, we begin to see the 'differences' in the light of these categories rather than respecting and embracing it.

Some partners even go to the extent of changing themselves as per the other person, thinking that it will help strengthen their relationship. While it may have worked for some, most people end up reaching a threshold where they break down, wondering about the point of all the sacrifices they've been making. In such situations, they begin to accuse the other partner for not recognizing and appreciating their adjustments, whereas the partner, who never made it a compulsion for them to change, continues to wonder how he/she is to be blamed for the breakdown.

In any given relationship, you cannot change the other person, however torturing that person is! You may be able to bring some behavioural changes but the core of their personality most often remains untouched. If you decide to bring about changes in yourself for someone else, it is your choice and decision. Saying that you did it for your partner's happiness is not going to undo the mistake you made. Hence, in any relationship, remember that the other person will always be different from you. Your beliefs, ideas, behaviour, values, perspectives, likes and dislikes will mostly be different from the other person. What is important between you and your partner is how you utilize each other's strength to make the relationship healthy rather than focusing all your energy on proving the other person wrong.

Rejoice the uniqueness that each one around you carries. Make an effort to understand their difference in light of respecting their perspective and focus your energy on bringing out more goodness in them. Highlight their strengths and bring out the best in them. Embrace differences with more generosity and empathy. Each time you feel that your friend/partner/

family should behave or react in a particular way, remind yourself that they are not you so they may not react the way you would.

Remember:

- Your parents/friends/partners are not wrong. They are just *different*.
- When someone's differences begin to frustrate you, understand their background. Perhaps you can sit with them and ask them about their childhood and the beliefs they grew up with. That will bring you closer to understanding why they react or behave in a certain way.
- We all walk around with an illusionary magical mirror and place it in between whenever we meet people. So the next time you feel you are criticizing a person or your mind tells you that he/she is wrong in their perspective, remember to remove the magical mirror. They are not your replica. They are different.
- Do not exhaust your energy in changing the person. Use the same energy in embracing the differences by respecting those.

Look for uniqueness in yourself and in everyone around you. It will then not be disappointing to find that each person is differently perfect in his/her own way.

12 | The Gratitude Way

"If you want to sleep more soundly, count blessings, not sheep."

- Dr. Emmons

When I was working with Eurokids, a chain of playschools for toddlers, I encountered many parents who literally forced their children to say 'Thank You', so that nobody points a finger at their parenting style. The poor child would then just utter these two words without even understanding the meaning of it. Since this conditioning gets only deeper with time, as adults, we often start regarding this 'expression of gratitude' as a formality and tag it under 'good manners'. This is not the only myth of gratitude; there are several others that can be listed:

- ***Gratitude is same as indebtedness***

  Many people feel obliged or are often forced to return a favor and consider that as a way of expressing gratitude. However, gratitude is not the same as indebtedness. Indebtedness often generates negative energy within us as it becomes an act of compulsion and not a behaviour that one executes with a feeling of joy, affection and willingness. A grateful person becomes naturally inclined to be grateful to everyone and everything around and not just to one or few benefactors.

- ***Gratitude must be practiced because it brings more material gains***

  Some people believe in this statement and begin to execute grateful attitude with an intention of acquiring more wealth in life. Each time they pretend to be grateful, it is with the intention of asking for more material gifts and success. Feeling of gratitude does not exist where its intention is forceful or attached to some gains - material or spiritual - in return. The feeling of gratitude experienced in the process matters and not the after effects of your gesture. Practicing it in everyday life brings more peace and more joy to your existence.

- ***If you don't practice gratitude, everything (all material gains) will be taken away by God***

  People who religiously follow this myth are the most fearful beings in life. These are the people who often pray to God because they fear that if they don't do this, they will be severely punished, put in hell or live a miserable life on this earth. It is said that 'fear' is an emotion that gets you *away* from God and 'love' is an emotion that takes you *closer* to the Supreme Being. So, gratitude practiced out of fear is not going to lead you anywhere; instead, it will make you more agitated in life. God is not an egoist who will get angry and take revenge by snatching away your needs and luxuries. Practice gratitude out of love and not fear.

- ***Practicing gratitude will end all your sufferings and pain***

  Nothing in this world will ever end the pain and sufferings or challenges. Those have been there since time immemorial and will continue to exist forever. The challenge is not to end the sufferings but to find peace and joy even in the time that is painful. Practicing gratitude calms your mind in such a way that at time of suffering, you are automatically reminded of multiple things in life that are wonderful. The pain and struggle remains, but your ability to deal with it gets strengthened.

So then, what IS gratitude?

Gratitude is an 'expression' of being content with anything that comes your way, or everything that you have in life. It is a form of expression that makes you feel good about what you are blessed with, and gets you closer to your inner self. It helps you keep the ego - I, me, and myself - aside. The ego often pulls you in the cycle of looking and judging everyone and everything around with the shades of superior and inferior. There are times when the ego demands self-appreciation ("I did this", "I made it possible") and though you may feel elated for a moment, the feeling of abundance will never touch your being. On the other hand, when you look at things, people and your own life with a grateful perspective, the feeling of abundance sets in. This feeling is a source of immense joy and it is not momentary. Gratitude is an act of feeling and being thankful for things and people that have been a part of your existence - your body, health, nature, food, shelter, clothing, work, education, loved ones and so on.

It is human nature to get trapped in the chain of 'taking things for granted'. The moment we fall in this trap, we step away from that feeling of abundance and begin to crave for more in life, without spending time to relish the good things. The more we begin to take things for granted, the more we begin to thicken the ego shield around us. Practicing gratitude is a way of thinning the ego shield and opening the door for happiness and peace to creep in.

Gratitude is not just about repeating the phrase 'Thank You'. Gratitude refers to the feeling within when these words are expressed. Imagine everything that you have right now in your life – all the basic necessities to the luxuries to every desire fulfilled. Make a list of all these things and include every single thing that contributes to your existence – your work, designation, money, home, family, food, clothes, foreign trips, fancy gadgets, internet, vehicles, natural beauty etc. List every single thing that you feel is a part of your existence.

Once you finish making that list, go through it one more time. Read every point carefully and add more if you remember something you may have missed. Re-read it again and this time, note what you feel about them. Is there a sense of happiness while you read it, or are you already comprehending 'what more can be gained and added to the list'? In case of the former, the ecstatic feeling you experience while reading the list is what can be termed as 'gratitude'. In case you experience the latter, imagine how you would feel if *everything* mentioned on that list is being taken away from you for two days. When you spend 48 hours without the things mentioned on that list, the 49th hour, when you get those back, will make you experience that ecstatic feeling and that is how it feels to be truly grateful in life.

Is it necessary to be grateful?

It is not mandatory for everyone to be grateful. It is a personal choice and this choice depends on how a person wishes to feel or live his/her life. Most often, people who aren't grateful are looked upon as being 'mean' or 'wrong' or 'horrible' human beings, but really, it is their personal choice to feel and act however they wish to! It is a part of their freewill. Just like happiness cannot be enforced on someone, gratitude cannot be forcefully attached to human nature. So, while gratitude is a sure shot way to experience bliss and happiness in life, it is not a mandatory virtue.

I wrote my gratitude list and I still don't feel better!
1. Alcohol to help me curb my pain.
2. Food to stuff my feelings with
3. Cigarettes to help me relieve my stress.

What happens when one is grateful?

Practicing gratitude balances our three vital states - physical, mental, emotional - and helps us experience the euphoric feeling without getting intoxicated. It has a direct effect on our physical health, psychological well-being, and on our relationships with others. The power of gratitude is mentioned in almost every scripture and has been practiced by men and women for decades now. After discovering the effect of gratitude in one's life, many scientists and neuroscientists have spent their time and energy researching on this powerful virtue, and some of the findings from these researches suggest that practicing gratitude offers many benefits, some of which include:

- Feel-good factor about 'self' and 'life'
- Increased levels of optimism
- Stronger and healthier immune system
- Immense peace and joy
- Strength during hard times
- Building up emotional strength
- Lesser complains about physical health (aches, high blood pressure, etc)
- Increased alertness, liveliness, generosity and compassion
- Keeping away from feelings of loneliness or depression

These are just some of the positive outcomes of practicing gratitude in your everyday life. While there are tons of articles available online to support the positive effect of gratitude, it is important to note that the feeling of gratitude works only when you are truly, with all your heart, grateful for something. Ask yourself, "What is that one thing in my life right now that I cannot live without?" Whatever the answer, notice how you feel with the thought of having that thing and notice how would you feel if that thing is taken away from you the very next minute. That one thing is your first thing to go on the gratitude wall/board/diary. While it may seem mechanical initially, you will soon begin to feel its effect on your mind.

How can you be more grateful?

Start with creating a gratitude journal, listing three things you are grateful for, usually before going to bed, and every day, add three new things to that list. It could be as simple as - 'I am grateful for functional legs, hands and eyes'. Each time you write a thing, imagine your life without it and the thankful feeling that you feel at that very moment is nothing but profound gratitude.

Take a Gratitude Walk

Whenever you feel low, stressed, worried or negative about life, take a gratitude stroll. Step out for a ten minute walk in a nearby park, office compound or the road. As you walk, notice the natural beauty around you, pay attention to everything that's contributing to that walk – healthy body, a pair of eyes to look around, your heart, your lungs that help you breathe as you walk, your ability to comprehend things (brain, senses, knowledge etc) and so on. With each item, let yourself breathe in that gift and breathe out the chaos that does not serve you. This exercise helps you convert your negative energies into positive vibes and leaves you with a sense of gratitude and compassion towards life.

Gratitude Box or Jar

Catch hold of an empty box or jar and label that as your gratitude box/jar. Each day, write one thing you are grateful about on a piece of paper, fold it and put it in the box. Make a habit of putting one paper everyday and fill up your gratitude box. The moments you feel low and upset, sit with this box and begin to read one paper at a time. This may not wash out your concerns but it will definitely give you the strength to sail though those tough times.

Gratitude Letter

If you feel you haven't been grateful enough to people around, especially friends or loved ones who have been with you in your rough times, grab a pen and paper and write to them. Even though many people would prefer email over writing, I encourage you to try writing a letter instead. Express your true feelings of gratitude in this letter mentioning everything that the person did to help you and how that made you feel. Once you finish writing your expression, deliver that letter to the person. Surprise them with a posted letter or hand it to them when you meet them. Stay there while they read it, or if you are comfortable, read the letter to the person. This form of expression will not only make you feel light but it will also be a source of immense joy, which will help you wipe out the feelings of loneliness.

Many people find it hard to practice gratitude because they become a victim to something known as the 'I lack' phenomenon. Each time they get something, their mind automatically drifts to other things that they can, or could have, possessed. For e.g. someone owns a single-door fridge in excellent working condition, but they want a new one, because they shifted to a bigger apartment and people were pointing out how a bigger fridge would look better. Someone might have a whole wardrobe full of clothes and yet feel that they lack good clothes. Each time you feel you 'lack' something, remind yourself that it is not a new thing that you need but a new perspective to see the existing abundance in your life. So, wear the glasses of fresh perspective and look around you and accept the things that you already have. You have everything that you need for your existence at this very minute!

Five things I am grateful for today:
→ That I did not burn my toast
→ I did not kill anyone while speeding the car.
→ That my boss did not behave like a jerk today.
→ That police did not catch me for driving without liscence
→ That one pimple is gone, and I am left with two more to go
I like your list better
→ Stars
→ Moon
→ Chocolates
→ Pajamas
→ Dora school bag

Creating 'Gratitude Badges'

Cut out a piece of paper and write – 'I am most grateful to you for ___________'. Write these to the people you wish to thank for anything you feel grateful for, and give it to them.

"Let us rise up and be thankful, for if we didn't learn a lot today, at least we learned a little, and if we didn't learn a little, at least we didn't get sick, and if we got sick, at least we didn't die; so, let us all be thankful" - Buddha

13 | The Art of Letting Go

"True forgiveness is when you can say, 'Thank you for that experience.'"

~ Oprah Winfrey

Holding a grudge or anger against someone who hurt you is a common human trait. From the time we are small, we get used to the term - 'forgive them' or 'forgive and forget'. We are taught that forgiveness is the key to a calmer and happier self. We take it into consideration whenever a situation arises, but it is only later in life when we reach an emotionally critical stage, like when someone cheats you as a friend or a lover, we realize that nobody taught us *how* to forgive and forget.

For a long time, I struggled to understand this 'how'. During that time, forgiveness to me meant completely ignoring the act or the person and freeing myself from it by making peace with the same person, but the moment I would begin to do that, I would end up reminding myself more about the hurt and pain caused by that person. I just couldn't let myself off the hook and come to terms with 'forgive and forget'. It seemed like it was easier said than done. It was a crazy idea to forgive and forget someone who damaged your whole being while you were busy trusting that person! I had many friends say, "you let it happen to yourself" or "you should have been more careful" and I felt like turning around and staring each one in the eye and say, "really? You think I am a lunatic who enjoys causing pain to my own self on purpose?"

I had a friend who was sexually abused as a child and the day she shared how horrendous her childhood was and how she was struggling to forget all of it, I began to question the whole aspect of 'forgiveness'. One, how could you forget such painful childhood experiences? Two, how and why on earth would you forgive the abuser and make peace with someone who tried to ruin you while you were young and naïve? It seemed insanely impossible to forget all of it at once and move on with life. So, while holding on to it seemed more painful, forgiving and forgetting seemed more like an 'end of the world' situation.

The more I tried to reason out the 'forgive and forget' principle, the more firmly I continued to hold on to the grudges within. I realized that this system wasn't working well for me or for my friends and I had to look for a way to get past the grudge, so with that determination, I began to look at forgiveness from a more realistic point of view. I began to formulate my own understanding of the term 'forgiveness'.

How can you practice forgiveness?

Forgiveness may not mean - completely and at once - forgiving or forgetting the person or an act, because the memory of what happened in the past will always be there with you in your mind and body. Forgiveness can mean having the painful memory but not being able to relive the pain and hurt all your life. So, the person or act is still there in your mind but if you can work on reducing its effect on yourself, that process can be called forgiveness. According to this understanding, I did not feel the stress and tension of forgetting everything all at once, and the focus was on reducing the hurt and pain being caused while reliving the memory. I went step by step, taking my own sweet time in reducing the intensity of the hurt and pain. Let me take the example of the friend who was sexually abused as a child and describe the process with these steps:

- Speak about the incident to a friend/counsellor/ confidante. Let it all out.
- Accept and embrace your emotions: Don't run away from what you are feeling. Accept that you were hurt and angry and that it was painful. Accept that you were vulnerable and unprepared for emotional outbreak coming your way. Don't fight the emotions because the more you fight or try to suppress it, the more it will continue to pop up. If the pain or anger goes beyond your ability to deal with it, seek a counsellor's help or at that very moment, take a piece of paper or a diary and write down whatever you are feeling/thinking. Writing is very therapeutic and often helps in dealing with repressed emotions.
- Bring your focus and energy back from external to internal: Remind yourself that in the past, when you were hurt, the focus was more on trusting the other person (external) and less on self-protection because you did not see it coming the painful way. Now, you are comparatively stronger and able to wrap a protective blanket around you, so bring your energy and divert it towards making yourself feel better, stronger, comfortable and happier. From 'I have to forgive and forget the other person', bring your attention to ways you can strengthen your inner self (by incorporating the ways listed in this book). This will help you build your inner strength and make you feel less vulnerable as a person. Remember, the times we feel weak, victimized and vulnerable, are the times where we experience the pain, hurt or anger all the more! In this process of strengthening the inner self, let yourself heal. The forgiveness and

forgetting process will automatically follow.

- Forgive yourself: Imagine a friend, filled with guilt, comes to you and tells you about a situation where you can clearly see that she is not at fault. How would you pacify that friend? The first thing you can do is listen to the problem and the moment the friend starts blaming herself, you may say, "Hey! Don't beat yourself up. It wasn't your fault. You were helpless or probably did not know what to do then! It is OK. Let it go."In this process of forgiveness, become your own best friend and remind yourself that it wasn't your fault that you trusted the person. You did not see it coming or maybe you did but you felt helpless then! So tell yourself that it is OK to have felt helpless because you were young and naïve. And for all of it, forgive yourself. Remind yourself that your mind, body and soul deserves love and affection more than anger and pain and in this process of being your own best buddy, forgive yourself for what happened in the past.
- Seek help: When we experience an emotional outburst or hurt, it becomes very difficult to wear a practical hat and replace it with the emotional hat. As human beings, we are conditioned to drown in the pool of emotions so many a times, even though we feel we are going the painful way, we become helpless and continue to walk the same path till we reach the level of emotional exhaustion. When there are situations in life where you find it difficult to forgive or forget the past painful instances, it is OK and healthy to seek professional help. A counsellor is equipped to help you reduce the intensity of pain, hurt

or anger and help you heal the deep emotional wounds. Seeking help is another way of walking the process of healing and forgiving.

- Breathe and exhale it out: The memory of a painful incident becomes challenging to erase, but its effect on you is what needs to be dealt with on a priority basis. As human beings, whatever we experience in life right from our early childhood, the memories get stored in our body. Your breath is one powerful way of helping you to release these stored painful body memories. Notice your breath as it is. Don't try to control it or breathe forcefully. Right now, as you read this, just bring your focus on your breath. Bring your focus on the rise and fall of your belly. Just notice your breaths – be aware that you are inhaling and exhaling, at whatever pace you feel comfortable.

- Inhale, fill your stomach in awareness and with the same awareness, exhale it out saying, 'I let it all go'. Inhale once again and while exhaling, in complete awareness, say, 'I let it all go'. You can either say it our loud when you are alone or just say it in your mind. Make this a rhythmic process between your breath and the 'let it all go' phrase. Tell yourself while exhaling that you are letting out everything that isn't serving you right or that's causing you pain, hurt, anger and suffering. Practice it as often, and wherever, you can. You may think of a particular incident or the person and exhale it out or you may think of general things that are causing you hurt and exhale it out. Your breathing is a powerful connection between your mind and body and between the body and external forces, so make use of it in releasing the discomfort, hurt or anger.

- It is OK to disconnect: It is OK to distant yourself physically and/or emotionally from the person or situation. Forgiveness does not mean that you have to be the best of buddies with that person and continue to share a strong emotional bond. If the person or the behaviour continues to affect you negatively, it is OK to walk away from it. Remember that your priority is to protect yourself than worrying about how the other person might feel or think. Disconnecting and practicing the ways of forgiveness will only give you strength to face the person or the situation in future without letting yourself get hurt or angry with the same intensity.

- Remember - It is a process: Forgiveness does not happen overnight or by attending a week or a month long workshop. It is a process, and like any other process, it needs time. A process is like climbing 100 steps, one step at a time, being aware of each step, and not thinking of the 100th step or the time when you will reach that 100th step. In climbing these steps, there may be times when you feel tired, painful and exhausted, but the joy and satisfaction will only be experienced when you successfully climb the 100th step and sit there for a while at peace with yourself. What matters is how you take care of yourself (not depending on another person to climb on your behalf) in that exhaustion and support yourself. It is OK to pause and take a break and once you feel energized a bit, start climbing once again.

The process of forgiveness will be initiated the moment you tell yourself, 'I have had enough of it. I can't take this pain anymore and I am ready to let it go'. Forgiveness is being able to think of the hurt or pain or the person five years later and still having a smile on your face for the person you have become. It is a process of reducing the intensity of hurt, pain, anger by strengthening your inner self and working towards letting it go – one step at a time.

A Buddhist Prayer of Forgiveness

If I have harmed anyone in any way
either knowingly or unknowingly
through my own confusions
I ask their forgiveness.
If anyone has harmed me in any way
either knowingly or unknowingly
through their own confusions
I forgive them.
For all the ways that I harm myself,
Negate, doubt, belittle myself,
Judge or be unkind to myself
Through my own confusions
I forgive myself.

14 Don't Postpone Your Happiness

"Happiness is not something you postpone for the future; it is something you design for the present."

~ Jim Rohn

I have come across many people who 'plan' their happiness. First, they connect happiness with materialistic gains and then begin to work towards achieving the same. I have a friend who has religiously devoted her life to her work. She constantly lives in the future, so her idea of happiness is always planned in the form of future events – 'I will be happiest when I retire and go on a long holiday', 'I will be most happy when I get a long work-break', 'I will be ecstatic when I find the right guy and marry him'. She had a long list of times and moments when she would feel happy and relaxed, all in either the past or the future. One day I asked her, "But what if, God forbid, you die tomorrow? How will you achieve that happiness post-retirement?"

"Such a bitch you are! I am not going to die so soon," she replied, throwing me a dirty look. Although she laughed it out then and there, the thought struck me deep. How can you be so sure of living the next day when you know for a fact that death could be sudden and is inevitable? How can you be so sure that you will begin to experience the joy of learning your favorite dance form two months later when you aren't even sure if you will survive the next two weeks?

Most often, I hear people say, "If I get this thing done then I would be happy" which can be translated into, "I can't be happy till the time I get that thing done". Once that particular task is achieved, you ask, "Are you happy now?" and the possible response is, "Oh! I am, *but* there's just this one, another thing and then it will all be done."

I had a colleague who wanted to settle down in Canada and each time we talked, he would sulk over the difficult life in India and how he would be thrilled if he gets the opportunity to move to Canada. It always began with, "Only if I get the Canada Visa, I will be so grateful". Luckily, he did get the Visa and when he came to give me the news, he said, "Now I just hope and pray I get a good job there. I will be *so* happy then!' Once the job was sorted and I asked him if he was happy there, he said, *"Haan yar, lekin ab bas PR jo jaaye,* (Yes, but let's just hope I get PR), I will be super happy!"

Each time we link happiness with an event which may or may not happen in the distant future, we shift our focus from present joys to distant worries. This is exactly how we begin to postpone happiness. Happiness is a feeling. A feeling is always in the present moment. It can be 'thought' in the past or future but it can be 'felt' only in the present.

Take a pen and a paper and answer these

questions for yourself. Be honest:

- Are you happy at this very moment? If your sentence pauses with a 'but', then the answer is 'no'.
- Make a list of things that make you happy.
    - Dancing
    - Cooking
    - A run in the park
    - ____________________
    - ____________________
    - ____________________
    - ____________________
    - ____________________
    - ____________________

Once you have made the list, for each item, ask yourself, "Am I doing (pick one thing at a time) what makes me happy?"

Incorporate what makes you happy in your life 'right now'. Your life is what is happening to you *now*. If you love sitting by the beach, do it now. If you want to experience happiness by dancing it out, do it now. If writing makes you feel happy, pick up a pen right away. Do what makes you happy every single day of your life. Look for happiness within and around you and feel it at that moment. While you are feeling happy for one thing, stay with it. Let it sink. Don't start thinking about the next thing that's going to make you happier.

15 Nothing Makes You Happy Unless 'Nothing' Makes You Happy

"Let everything happen to you, Beauty and terror; Just keep going, No feeling is final"

~ Rainer Maria Rilke

Once I was sitting and whining to my friend over how I am doomed in life when it came to finances. I was twenty-eight and had no savings of my own! While I was complaining about how money has always been a concerning factor in my life, she asked me, "Was there ever a time when you were without any money, could not afford to eat and had no place to live in?"

I was puzzled by that question because she and I both knew that I had never faced such a situation. I quickly shook my head and said, "No. Thankfully, I have never reached that point."

She smiled and continued, "Were you content when your salary was double the salary you are getting now?" My previous job was a well-paying one that I had left to continue working in the field of psychology.

I thought for a while and answered truthfully, "Yes, I think I was."

"So how come you continue to complain about that job?"

"Because I was not happy there! At that point, earning wasn't my concern. I was not satisfied with my job."

"But even with that salary amount, were you able to save?" she probed further.

"No," I said, wondering why I did not manage to save when I could have done it. I did not live a lavish lifestyle or spend unnecessarily on impulse shopping, partying and other leisure pastimes; yet I was left with zero savings.

"Shama," she said, "it will never be enough how much ever you earn, because every time you get a certain amount, you will have that many things to take care of and it will always seem less."

"But now when I look back, I feel that was enough," I tried to reason with my vulnerable ego.

"It will never be enough unless you let yourself have what you have and find happiness and contentment in it."

"And how exactly do I do that?" I enquired.

"By not cribbing about what has gone and by not dreaming about what isn't happening right now. Right now, with whatever you have, learn to be happy with it. If you have Rs 200 with you today, stay with it. Be happy that you have what you need at this precise moment. Let yourself have those 200 bucks rather than wondering how things would have been better if you had Rs 2000 instead!"

I thought about what my friend had just said and wondered if I let myself have what I have in my life. I realized that not just with money, I executed that behaviour with everything in my life! I did not let myself have my morning *chai* because I was focused on planning my day. I did not let myself admire my beautiful house because I was busy worrying about other non-existent futuristic things. I had almost everything a person would need to feel blessed and yet I never paused for a moment to let myself have - enjoy, nurture, be happy with - what I had in life.

We all at some point or the other get into the mode of complaining and cribbing about life, either one, or its various aspects. We get busy worrying about the missing things and let go of our chances to enjoy what we have at hand! Pause for a while from that never-ending rat race and ask yourself, "Do I let myself have what I have?"

If your salary is less than the standard expectation, let yourself have that before dreaming and desiring a higher amount. If your apartment is small, let yourself have that before you get busy investing and buying a bigger one. For a moment, stay with what is there in your life right now! Breathe in all the possible needs that are already being met in your life!

When I asked my friend, "But won't this make me lazy and put me in my comfort zone of not aiming for a better life?" she calmly replied, "your comfort zone will never be defined. Once you manage to acquire what you have in mind right now, the moment you reach that stage, another dream, a higher version of that achievement, will be awaiting your mind's doorstep and you will then continue to walk the never-ending path of constantly living in the future. No, it will not make you lazy and less determined. It will only make you more grateful and humble in life. It will make you less anxious and cause lesser stress in life and this will only make you a positive person. So when I say let yourself have what you have, I mean be happy and grateful for what is already in your life and cherish that. Only when you are able to cherish it with immense joy and satisfaction, you will reach a point where it will always be enough!"

Since that day, I made this a mantra in my life. There are days when I worry if I will be left with money to pay my bills in the next 20 days and precisely at those moments, I bring myself back to the present and let myself have the cup of *chai* in front of me. I let myself have the comfortable house I live in and I let myself have every single thing in my life which I did not have before and that I am blessed to have now! The more I practice this in my life, the less anxious it makes me. I am able to focus more on things at hand and give my 100 % rather than feeling stressed about things I may encounter in the future.

Once you make this statement a mantra in your life, you will often find yourself getting in touch with the happiness that is hard to define. You want to try it? Do this: buy yourself a chocolate, or any dish that you love, and keep it in front of you. Take one piece of it in complete awareness and put it in your mouth. Take in the aroma of it and relish as it touches every taste bud in your mouth. Close your eyes for few seconds and let your entire focus be on the taste of that piece of chocolate. Eat it as slowly as you can, savoring every bit of it. This is exactly how you let yourself have what you have – by savoring and relishing every bit of the thing available to you right now.

Most of the time, we do want things but we don't let ourselves have it. You may crave for a bar of chocolate but the moment it is in your hand and you begin to eat it, you shift your focus on the next thing in your mind – dinner plans, office work, conversation with a friend etc. It is very rare that you let yourself enjoy its aroma and bring your attention to how delicious it tastes and how heavenly it feels when the chocolate melts inside your mouth. You get busy wanting the next piece of chocolate and forget about what is already in your mouth.

Some people go to the extent of thinking they will be happy if they reach a level where they see other people operating. For instance, if you see someone with a fancy job, a sea-facing bungalow and a hot girlfriend, you are most likely to assume that this person is the luckiest and happiest human being and you begin to chase that happiness, making it your own dream. Unfortunately, when you reach that destination, after a long and painful struggle, you are most likely to have other dreams already planned to be chased and left with no time to enjoy what you really get. Your whole life is then spent chasing something new and wanting to reach *there* and not having a day's time to pause to let yourself enjoy what you have.

Wanting something is different from having something. While *wanting* is always set in the future, *having* is focused on the present. The *wanting* will always make you feel more hungry, restless, agitated and anxious. When we don't take in the good things that are already there in our lives, we begin to feel that we don't have enough. So look around and see what you already have and spend time taking that in. Touch it, feel it, savor it and breathe with it so that the next time your mind tells you, 'you don't have enough', your focus is automatically shifted to the goodness you already have in your life.

Tip:

Make it a habit. Consciously practice this every day. To make it easier, you can start with food – each time you eat anything, follow the steps of letting yourself have it. Don't just mechanically let it be a hand-mouth action. Spend time savoring the food item. While it may seem like a task initially, it will feel more calm and comforting when the conscious practice becomes a part of your everyday functioning.

16 Be Wise, Nature Wise

"Take hold of your own life. See that the whole existence is celebrating. These trees are not serious, these birds are not serious. The rivers and the oceans are wild, and everywhere there is fun, everywhere there is joy and delight. Watch existence, listen to the existence and become a part of it."

~ Osho

Once I was travelling back from a seminar in a friend's car and it started to drizzle. A colleague sitting in the backseat began to roll up the window on her side, but I began to roll down my side of the window. My friend, who was driving the car, wondered what I was up to and that's when I turned around and said, "I am sorry in advance for dirtying your car seat, but you can get it cleaned when you give it for servicing." I put my head out, letting the raindrops fall on my face, and on my clothes and on the car seat, and for the next half hour, I was disconnected from all the worries and problems that life had in store for me.

The duo sitting in the car definitely labeled me as a 'mad woman' but what I experienced then was a feeling I cannot even begin to describe in words. I let my whole focus be on enjoying the beauty all around. While my colleague was busy focusing on how dirty the roads have become with potholes everywhere, noise pollution, air pollution and traffic on the road, I was lost in admiring the green trees on the sidewalk, the colorful flowers which I had not seen in years, the cloudy sky which was vast and empty, (unlike the traffic on the road), and the birds making their way home or finding shelter on the nearest tree cozying up together to feel warm. For those thirty minutes, I got busy feeling myself brim with positive energy.

'Nature' is one of the most powerful ways of reminding us that our existence is beautiful. As human beings, we begin to define life as challenging, tough, painful, time-bound, competitive, and an unavoidable struggle. As we get busy living this definition of life every single day, we start attracting all possible negative emotions or energy that prevent us from experiencing peace and happiness. Some of us become aware of the universal beauty and spend time in connecting with it, but there are many who regard it as sheer wastage of time, energy and intelligence. I have had people say 'admiring nature? I would rather spend time working on finishing a code, getting a promotion and earning more money'. People who fall in this 'others' category are often the ones who will be found complaining about everything in their life, from their food to work to children to clothes to seasons to government to water supply and so on.

Take a moment and ask yourself, "Do I feel I am getting trapped in the *complaint cyclone*?" If yes, close this book for a while, get up and go to the nearest window, balcony or terrace and look at the sky. Once you are out, or get a view of the natural world, start noticing anything and everything you can find in nature – sky, birds of all kinds, trees, flowers, clouds, nests, animals, the sun, the moon, stars, the sea, beach sand, shells etc. If you decide to walk on the ground, observe the grass beneath (remove your footwear and feel the grass), notice the small insects, ants, the dew drops, the tiny plants growing out of nowhere. If it is raining where you are, just get your hand out, and if you can afford to step out in the rain for few seconds, there's nothing like it! Experience the drops touching your skin. For the next five-ten minutes, let your whole focus and attention be on the beauty that nature has to offer.

As you observe the beauty around, breathe in the abundant beauty and breathe out the chaos inside you. Especially if you are sitting in office and feel pressurized with work, step out for five minutes and spend that time observing the natural beauty around. For people who get up and stand against a glass window to admire the rain, make an effort to step out and *feel* the raindrops instead. You will notice the difference yourself. Each time you spend time admiring nature, your mind may poke its nose and continue to remind you, 'you are wasting your time'. Don't fight this thought. Your mind is not used to relaxing and finding happiness in small and little things, so it will fight back each time it sees your focus being diverted to natural happiness. Notice the thoughts, the agitation, the unease, while you spend time admiring nature and each time you become aware of this agitation, acknowledge it and bring your focus back to nature. Bring your focus on your breaths and lose yourself in the beauty that nature has in store.

Nature has a therapeutic effect on our mind and body. It has the power of rejuvenating every cell and making us feel alive and positive. This can happen only if *we* let it happen. Only when *we decide* to open our arms to it, it will show us its abundant beauty and power of healing. Make a habit of spending at least ten minutes every day observing, admiring and getting in touch with nature. While you are walking, driving (especially when you are stuck in traffic), holidaying, sulking, hurting, boiling with anger, bring your focus and attention to nature and notice every bit of what you see around you.

In many scriptures and philosophical books, nature is also regarded as a powerful way of teaching us the hidden secrets of life. The behaviours that we secretly desire to inculcate within – how to be more patient, how to be a good listener, how to be compassionate, how to fight tough situations etc – every answer to these questions can be found in nature and the key to this is observation and time. When you make efforts and give time to learn, it will teach you well.

Herman Hesse in his book *Siddhartha* talks about the power of nature in helping a person attain peace and happiness. In one of the sections, a character - a ferryman named Vasudeva - talks to the protagonist Siddhartha about the power of *River* and how it taught him everything about life and made him wiser and happier.

Tenderly, he looked into the rushing water, into the transparent green, into the crystal lines of its drawing, so rich in secrets. Bright pearls he saw rising from the deep, quiet bubbles of air floating on the reflecting surface, the blue of the sky being depicted in it. With a thousand eyes, the river looked at him, with green ones, with white ones, with crystal ones, with sky-blue ones. How did he love this water, how did it delight him, how grateful was he to it! In his heart he heard the voice talking, which was newly awaking, and it told him:

Love this water! Stay near it! Learn from it! Oh yes, he wanted to learn from it, he wanted to listen to it. He who would understand this water and its secrets, so it seemed to him, would also understand many other things, many secrets, all secrets.

"You will learn it," spoke Vasudeva, "but not from me. The river has taught me to listen, from it

you will learn it as well. It knows everything, the river, everything can be learned from it. See, you've already learned this from the water too, that it is good to strive downwards, to sink, to seek depth. The rich and elegant Siddhartha is becoming an oarsman's servant, the learned Brahman Siddhartha becomes a ferryman: this has also been told to you by the river. You'll learn that other thing from it as well."

..."This it is," said Siddhartha. "And when I had learned it, I looked at my life, and it was also a river, and the boy Siddhartha was only separated from the man Siddhartha and from the old man Siddhartha by a shadow, not by something real. Also, Siddhartha's previous births were no past, and his death and his return to Brahma was no future. Nothing was, nothing will be; everything is, everything has existence and is present."

Siddhartha spoke with ecstasy; deeply, this enlightenment had delighted him. And time after time, his smile became more similar to the ferryman's, became almost just as bright, almost just as thoroughly glowing with bliss, just as shining out of thousand small wrinkles, just as alike to a child's, just as alike to an old man's.'

The life-force, God, *Prana*, Universe, Supreme Intelligence, however you relate to it, resides in this nature. The moment you spend time connecting with nature, you let yourself connect with that copious life-force. This life energy has the ability to heal and provide peace and happiness in your existence. The more you connect with it and let it inside your system, the more happy and peaceful you will feel within. That doesn't mean that if you have a problem, you step out in nature and wait for it to perform magic on your mind and body. Observing nature means leaving your intellect, knowledge, and thoughtful mind away and enjoying it without any aims, goals or end result in mind. Making nature your love and lover will only strengthen your heart further and once you experience this, your definition of life will change from being 'chaotic' to 'effortless effort'.

My Nature Space

Think of the most beautiful, natural place you've ever visited. Stick a picture of it in a special notebook. If possible, try to imagine and re-live that experience in your memory and draw it in that notebook. It doesn't matter how well or bad you draw. What matters is how well you can remember the details – the colors, shapes, sizes, etc - of the place. Reliving the moment will automatically have a soothing effect on your body and mind. Paint it out or photograph it. Fill that special notebook with 'nature spaces' not just today but once every four-six days. Stay connected with nature as often as you can and in as many different ways as you can. This will flood your heart and mind with peace and happiness.

Tips:

- Go cycling at least once a week, preferably on early mornings.
- Go hiking or trekking once in a few months.
- Spend ten minutes every day in open space,

under the sky.

- Walk barefoot on the earth – feeling the sand/mud/grass beneath – at least once in two weeks.
- Touch or dip your legs in flowing water at least once in a few months.
- Listen to the chirping of birds *every day*.
- Notice and admire the moon, stars and/or sun at least every alternate day, for five minutes.

17 | The Smile Therapy

"Sometimes your joy is the source of your smile, but sometimes your smile can be the source of your joy."

~ Thích Nhất Hạnh

As we walk around or sit and work at our office desk, we are constantly filled with stress, anxiety and worries. This stress-energy begins to crawl from our forehead to down our toes, tensing each muscle of our body. It often gets accumulated in certain parts of our body causing us physical ache, usually in the back, head, neck or legs. We get conditioned to pop a pill when we experience such aches but the cycle of stress energy accumulating in our body continues to move each day. The first point where the stress energy usually gets accumulated is the forehead, especially the part between the eyebrows. As you read these lines, notice if your facial muscles are tensed or relaxed. Notice if the region between your eyebrows tends to stiffen while you are doing a certain task. If you notice that your facial muscles are most often tensed, practicing the smile therapy can work wonders in your life.

Smiling has a powerful ability to turn the negative energy into a positive one. We all tend to get attracted and wish to be closer to people who smile more than people who act grumpy all the time. The moment you are with someone who wears a smile on his/her face, note that your spirits automatically get lifted and you feel rejuvenated. Their smile is usually contagious and you often find yourself in a half-full smile just by looking at them. Smiling helps a person relax his body muscles and ease out the stress and tension he/she has been carrying throughout. It is one of the ways to experience peace, tranquility and happiness within.

Rule No. 1:

Smile for yourself

Smile because you want to smile and not just because your boss or husband or wife will be happy to see a smile on your face. As Ketut Lier in Elizabeth Gilbert's *Eat, Pray, Love* says, 'Smile with face, smile with mind, and good energy will come to you and clear away dirty energy. Even smile in your liver.' Relax those tensed facial muscles even as you read this book and wear a half or full smile. Wear a half smile each time you drink a cup of coffee or sit by the window admiring nature. Smile with each and every part of your body as if every cell inside your body is rejoicing for reasons unknown to you.

Each time you notice the facial muscles contracting, ease the frown and loosen up the tensed muscles. Wear a half smile almost all the time. No, people will not label you as a lunatic and even if they do, consider them as ignorant who are yet to discover the power of a smile. When you smile for yourself, i.e. with all your heart and mind, you begin to transform the negative energy within and around you into a positive one. When I say 'smile' here, I am referring more to the loosening of those tensed facial muscles. Ease them every day, for as long as you can and notice the difference in your mood. Once you begin to practice this rule in your life, you will gradually begin to feel calm and elated from within. Smile to feel happiness from the inside. Smile to make yourself happy because you, as much as the others, need and deserve your smile.

Rule No. 2:

Smile in Awareness

As you read these lines, bring your awareness on to your breaths. Notice the rise and fall of your stomach, and loosen up every tensed facial muscle, especially the frown between your eyebrows. Relax every inch of your facial features and let your lips turn into a gentle half curve. Feel the lightness on your face and each time you feel lighter, increase the curve on your lips. Smile with all your being because your smile is a profound source of the boundless happiness.

Rule No. 3:

Don't wait for a reason to smile

We have become experts in waiting for a reason or an occasion to execute things which can make us happy. We wait for our birthdays or marriage to feel special, we wait to hear jokes to laugh our lungs out, we wait for the drums to roll to dance to our heart's content. We love to wait for 'someday' to make things happen. Don't wait for any reason to smile. And if you can't survive without any reason, become the reason for your smile. Let your existence become the most profound reason for you to smile. When you begin to smile for your existence, it becomes a part of you and a source of immense happiness.

Rule No. 4:

Your smile will always work

This is a tried and tested fact. The more you smile around people, the more they will fall in love with your presence. When you smile with all your heart, you automatically ease out the burden from your shoulder and that can be felt in your presence by other people. When you smile and interact with a person, your work will almost always see the bright light. This doesn't mean you don't prepare your presentation and go in front of your boss and smile and he will be more than pleased to give you a salary raise! Smiling is not a substitute. It is an added flavor to everything that you do in your life. So catch hold of your smile and use it everywhere you go and in whatever you do.

Rule No. 5:

Do not label your smile as good or bad

I wonder who created this whole concept of categorizing a smile under good and bad. Please note that your smile, anyone's smile, can never, ever be categorized or judged. Smile is always just a smile. It is always positive. Neither good nor bad, but positive. And it is always healthy. Your smile is your asset and will always be, whether or not you believe it. It is what adds beauty to your beautiful existence. To me, something that adds life to your existence can never be classified under good and bad. It is always positive and worth cherishing. So value your smile. It is always gorgeous and it will always bring peace and happiness within.

As human beings, we are all constantly on guard every minute of our lives. We often let go of these walls only in the presence of our loved ones. We also assume that smiling is a way of letting go of this protective shield we manage to build around us. That's why you would see many people staring you down with an expressionless face. I have personally come across so many people, especially when I travelled in Mumbai locals, who would look at me with great surprise if I smiled at them when we had eye contact. It was almost as if the person is threatened by the smile. And that's when I would notice the guarded energy all around them. It was as if I could see the tension, burden and worry on their face while they continued to increase that stress even as I smiled at them.

People have changed the whole meaning of this concept with time. A smile is not a gesture that someone makes to indicate that he/she is sexually interested in you. If someone smiles at you, it might be purely because they recognize you as fellow human beings and not because they want to give you some secretive signal of being physically, sexually, emotionally or mentally interested in making love to you. The more we label and try to study this gesture, the more we lose out on its true meaning and purpose. To me, smile is just a simple yet profound gesture of recognizing that divine force of living existence within each one of us. It has no meaning beyond this whatsoever. So, smile without attaching any judgments or perceptions. Smile for your being and smile when you cherish others' existence.

I personally love to make people smile. I love to communicate to people how they look gorgeous with smiles on their face and how it suits them the best. While you continue to follow the above steps, do not hesitate in passing this smile bug to others. Just let them know that their smile is beautiful, that their whole appearance is magnificent with that smile on their face. This way, you become a profound source of joy not just for yourself but also for people around.

18 | *Take a Stand... and stick to it!*

"Staying silent is like a slow growing cancer to the soul and a trait of a true coward. There is nothing intelligent about not standing up for yourself. You may not win every battle. However, everyone will at least know what you stood for—you."

~ Shannon L. Alder

From what I've observed, every second person has this concern that they cannot say 'NO' to anyone, especially their loved ones. Many books have been published on this topic and there are psychologists who have dedicated their time and life in understanding and researching this concept. There are endless articles and reading material online to explain this phenomenon and many companies have made it compulsory to include this topic as a part of their team-building exercises. Since most of us are techno savvy and have already dedicated our lives to Google, I am going to skip the basic start of defining the concept of assertiveness.

In Indian culture, we are taught from a very young age to obey the elders and respect people around. Being nice to them, being good to them and being available to them for help are considered as the most important virtues. At any given time, if, as a child, we fail to meet other's needs, we are regarded as a 'bad child'. Even sometimes when the child is not in a mood to meet people, we force him/her to do so and ask him to keep a smile on his face and say hello to everyone. If the child denies this social ritual, he/she is scolded by the parents and labeled as an indiscipline child. When the child is growing up, the people around, especially family members, consciously and unconsciously begin to send the message across, through their behaviour and actions, that if the child doesn't do something as per someone else's wish, he/she is hurting the other person. E.g. If a mother has some work and asks her son to do it and if the son refuses because he's working on some school project, the mother would say, 'Yes, now even you say no to me and don't help me with my work. I am your mother, not your girlfriend, so why would you help me! You will learn to value me once I go away. Then you won't have anyone to ask you for help.' In simple words, such behaviour is referred to as 'emotional *atyachaar*'. Sometimes in such situations, the child begins to *feel guilty within for hurting* the mother and concludes that every time he says *no* to something, he/she is hurting the other person, and *if he/she continues to say no, the mother (or any loved one) may go away from him/her (fear of losing).*

As we grow old, this belief begins to sink even deeper into our psyche and without our realization, we reach a point where being assertive becomes the most tedious task in our lives. The moment we encounter a situation where we wish to say no, we hear two sirens – You are hurting/upsetting the other person and, You might end up losing the other person. In both cases, the concluding message is – 'It is *not* OK to say NO.'

Another learning we derive from our early childhood days is to make others happy i.e. *place other people's needs above ours*. A girl, right from an early age, is taught to take care of others - the family, the extended family, the husband, the in-laws, etc. Only when she succeeds in doing this, she is regarded as an ideal or perfect woman. And since we all love to run the rat race of achieving perfection, we continue to bear the pain internally. The same girl when she gets married is most likely to develop an innate *need of pleasing everyone around* and then, even if there are times when she is sick or feeling low and doesn't wish to do a certain thing, she ends up saying yes to the task, even if she wishes to say a loud NO.

Why is it important to learn to say no?

According to me, it is almost necessary to say 'No'. When you express assertiveness, you automatically put your needs above the other (please note that this is not same as being selfish). Assertive behaviour helps you break the cycle of pleasing everyone else at all levels and brings your focus back to your well-being. It reminds you that you have to take care of your needs as much as you love to care for others. It is also important to learn to say no to avoid being a doormat in the relationship and later chanting mantras like, "Why does it always happen to me?" or "*Mein kitna bhi karu sab k liye, hamesha kamm hi hota hai*" and so on. If you don't take the charge to stand up for yourself, nobody else will! And expecting others to understand without you making an effort to express and assert is like banging your head against the wall and blaming the wall for not comforting you.

When you attempt to say no, the other person usually makes you feel that you are the worst friend, wife, husband, daughter, son, partner, ever on this earth. This is because of the whole principle of 'if you are keeping me happy, you are a good human being'. Also, because you have been telling them 'yes' for years, they aren't used to hearing a 'no' from you, so they are bound to react with shock or throw an emotional bomb at you. There may be a possibility that the person might understand your reasons of saying a 'no' or there may be a situation where the person might get distant from you because of anger or ego. In the latter case, it is solely your decision to choose between continuing to please that person or finding another person who would respect your choice and still love you.

Assertiveness can never be forced on people. Even if my best friend or my partner is passive and I see them struggle because of this nature, I cannot transform them from a passive person to an assertive person. It is a personal choice. And the moment you decide to become assertive and break the 'being a doormat' trap, you have already taken the first step towards your wellbeing.

Rules of assertiveness:

- It is OK to say NO: It is OK to say no for things that you are not comfortable doing. It can be anything – saying no to a drink, a smoke, an extra serving of food, dance, a drive, a picture etc.
- It is OK to put your needs over others: If you are strong, you can strengthen others. If you become weak, you will only end up being more frustrated and get a feeling of 'being used'.
- By saying a NO, you don't hurt the other person: If others get hurt, it is their perception. You don't become responsible for how they choose to feel in life. If the person abandons you, do not take the blame on yourself (especially if you genuinely couldn't be there and said a 'no'). What matters here is that you spoke and stood for yourself and that is courageous, necessary and worthy in the long run.
- The more you say 'yes' (when you wish to say a loud 'no'), the more dependency you create for the other person: I have come across so many housewives who complain that how much ever they do for their family, it is never enough.

In therapy, there are women saying that their husbands rarely appreciate the work they do, and the sacrifices they make. When I ask them, "Who told you to travel that extra mile and please your family members?" they answer, "no one." When I ask them if anyone forced them to make those sacrifices, the answer is the same. So I gently tell them, "Well, if you keep saying yes for everything all the time, how will a person get to know that you are not comfortable doing certain things?" To this, they conveniently say, "But they should understand this, *na*!" And I continue, "*Na*, my dear. They will never understand. No one can ever understand without you communicating it to them. This is like handing your locker keys to your loved ones and then getting annoyed because they use the keys to open your safe and browse through your personal items all the time!"

If you aren't comfortable doing certain things, communicate. Continuing to do it and expecting the other person to understand and respect your sacrifices is futile. So instead of waiting for forty-fifty years to reach a point where you feel you are always being used or taken for granted, begin to say 'no'. Start expressing your disagreement – not with an intention to put the other person down or teach a lesson to someone, but with an intention of making the other person understand your genuine wish and to arrive at a win-win solution.

PS: Giving a silent treatment to you partner or friend or boss will never, ever communicate what you intend to. Instead, it is definitely going to make the matter worse.

Tips:

- Take baby steps: Practice saying 'no' at places where the emotional threat is less. E.g. do not give in when any salesman forces you to buy something you do not want, even if he/she gives you emotional reasons that will most likely melt your heart. Continuously repeat a statement conveying your true emotions. Repeating a request affirms your viewpoint and keeps the discussion focused. Be clear on what you want and accept a compromise only if you are happy with the settlement.
- Practice saying 'no' with conviction in front of a mirror: Do it several times before going to say that to someone in person. Mirroring the dialogues always helps in gaining your strength and increases your will to express your needs. Imagine the person standing on the other side of the mirror and speak as if you are actually having a dialogue with that person. Remember the statements and stick to the point – saying 'No'. Repeat till you begin to feel a little confident and become convinced about saying a no and not giving up to the situation/person.
- Practice saying no with someone who understands: E.g. if you have to say 'no' to your superior for some work, practice saying 'no' with your best friend, or any trusted person, before you stand in front of the superior and execute assertive behaviour. Let them become the

superior and instruct them to even act like one. Keep your focus on strengthening your words and the body language.

- Use affirmations or positive statements to replace the negative ones: E.g. if your friend keeps borrowing money from you and you feel hesitant or bad for saying no to the request, tell yourself that it is OK to not loan money to a friend when you yourself are putting an effort in making yourself financially independent. (You can create your own positive statements)
- Use 'I' statements while expressing: This does not make the other person feel threatened and conveys your needs directly. For e.g. avoid saying – "You have no idea what I feel in life. My life has become a mess and all you do is sit in front of the computer and pretend to work!" Instead, you can say, "I feel exhausted dear/(name of the person). I need more help in managing kitchen and raising the kids at the same time."
- Agree to disagree: Remember that having a different point of view doesn't mean you are right and the other person is wrong or vice versa. If your friend suggests a South Indian restaurant which you hate, suggest another place you would wish to go and communicate that you dislike that place even though you agreed to go there several times in the past.
- While you try to be assertive in certain situations and expect the other person to understand your needs, you might also want to consider executing the same behaviour when someone else is telling you a 'no' for something you want them to do.

19 Power of Mindfulness

"I've told them that if each one can meditate an hour each day, that's good, but it's nowhere near enough. You've got to practice meditation when you walk, stand, lie down, sit, and work, while washing your hands, washing the dishes, sweeping the floor, drinking tea, talking to friends, or whatever you are doing. While washing the dishes, you might be thinking about the tea afterwards, and so try to get them out of the way as quickly as possible in order to sit and drink tea. But that means that you are incapable of living during the time you are washing the dishes. When you are washing the dishes, washing the dishes must be the most important thing in your life. Just as when you're drinking tea, drinking tea must be the most important thing in your life. When you're using the toilet, let that be the most important thing in your life. And so on. Chopping wood is meditation. Carrying water is meditation. Be mindful twenty four hours a day, not just during the one hour you may allot for formal meditation or reading scriptures and reciting prayers. Each act must be carried out in mindfulness."

– Thich Nhat Hanh

The 28th Rule (of Love) of Shams Tabriz[5] says, "The past in an interpretation. The future is an illusion. The world does not move through time as if it were a single line, proceeding from the past to the future. Instead time moves through and within us, in endless spirals. Eternity does not mean infinite time, but simply timelessness. If you want to experience eternal illumination, put the past and the future out of your mind and remain within the present moment." Time is said to be created by humans to make things convenient for fellow human beings. Ironically, this is the most inconvenient convenience ever created by mankind. To make things simple, the time was divided into seconds, minutes, hours, days, weeks, months, years and so on. This was further simplified by adding the terms past, present and the future. This simple act is solely responsible for most of the miseries ever experienced by mankind through centuries.

Right from a very young age, we are taught to plan and prepare ourselves for the future. And after being trained for this planning for almost two to three decades, we are then given messages such as 'be in the moment', 'live the present like you are going to die tomorrow' and so on.

The conditioning of staying in the past and future is extremely deep in each one of us and that is what, according to me, is the biggest cause of all our worries, anger, stress, anxiety, guilt, shame and fear. We are taught to treasure and hold on to these babies but were never taught how to make peace with them and live in the 'here and now'.

It wasn't until the beginning of 2014 that I came across this concept. I had heard every possible saying about living and enjoying the moment, and specially the one - 'live today as if you are going to die tomorrow' - which is almost said like an affirmative anthem in our culture. While I did hear them, I never got the *time* to ponder over it because I was extremely busy living the life of shame, guilt, fear, anger and disappointments. Though I heard the importance of living in the moment, nobody taught me 'how' to do that. And especially people who kept preaching these sayings went mum when I would ask them, 'how?' It was later that I realized that it was I who needs to find the 'how' and not wait for the knowledge to ascend while I continue to get trapped in the 'time cyclone'.

The need for this phenomenon came because I wanted to let go of everything from my body and life that did not serve me right. And doing that is the toughest task for all of us. I came across a friend who introduced me to the practical aspects of this concept and taught me some of the basic techniques to practice living in the moment. After practicing it for months now, I can vouch for its success and positive effect on your being. But, before I go ahead and share these techniques, it is important to understand that this phenomenon has, for centuries, benefitted human beings to attain inner happiness and peace of mind. Even though it is a tried and tested concept, it will appeal and affect only those who wish to make efforts in understanding and practicing it. It is not possible to do it for one day for five minutes and give up saying, "It's all fart and no shit". So before you conclude and label this concept as 'good or bad' or 'right or wrong', know what it is. Why is it important to be in the present? Introspect your behavioural and mental system and then choose to practice it. *With patience.*

What is 'Mindfulness' or 'Being in the Present'?

Mindfulness, in simple terms, means being completely and consciously aware of the present moment, i.e. being aware of anything and everything that you are doing at that very second.

Your thoughts have the ability to rush you in the past or in the future. Because we have been used to this travel since time immemorial, it becomes difficult to hold our focus in the present. However, mindfulness isn't about de-cluttering your mind and focusing on one thing. It is about being aware of the chaos within and outside. The practice of mindfulness will not magically remove all your worries, but it will help you understand the cause and effect of the same and thus, help you manage your own self in a healthier way.

Mindfulness is about letting yourself have what you have at this very moment, be it in thoughts or in action. For e.g. a practitioner of mindfulness will have the *chai* when he is having the *chai*. He will become aware of the aroma of the *chai*, the color of the *chai*. He will let himself relax for those five minutes and be in the moment of drinking that *chai*. In the process if he gets thoughts of the future, he will notice those thoughts and each time the mind wanders, he will try to bring his focus back to the cup of *chai* in his hand.

Being present in the moment means being consciously aware of all that is! When you are in this conscious state of awareness, it means you are accepting everything as it is. You are not in denial about your thoughts and emotions. It means that you are letting yourself feel and experience things without avoiding them or pushing them in the past or the future. Being in the moment means you aren't letting the negativity get rooted in your body, mind and soul - your whole being. You begin to accept your experiences, feelings, thoughts as you live each moment. Thus, not accumulating it within and then distributing it to past and future. It is when you gradually begin to make peace with your past and develop immunity to the non-existent future.

Why is it important?

In today's competitive world, we have become like robots, constantly in a rush to do something absent-mindedly or reach somewhere. We run without being aware of the fact that we are running. Anything that has to do with pausing or stopping for a while is considered a waste of time or unproductive. And to make all our actions productive, we conveniently include the so-called de-stressing exercises in this mad rat race. For all those who think taking one hour of time for yoga is highly impossible and futile, might try to include five minutes of something known as workplace yoga while their mind is completely focused on the next big meeting. We become experts in doing five things at a time and yet manage to have space to include several tasks in that moment. When we do this, our mind gets the liberty to multiply the existing chaos in our head. This results in all possible mental and emotional breakdowns. The thoughts and feelings of past creates miseries, hurt, pain, anger, guilt, shame and many such feelings that make us weak and vulnerable. Similarly, the thoughts of the non-existent future create uncertainties, fear, anxiety, frustration, doubts and other related emotions that always keep us on our guard.

Ask yourself, "What are the constant feelings/ thoughts I get throughout the day?" Once you get a response to this question, see if the response is associated with the past or future. Almost every unpleasant thought or emotion has its roots in either the past or the future. Now, ask yourself, "Do I have everything that I need at this very second?" The answer to this question will almost always be a "Yes". We always have what we need to survive in the present but because of the constant desire of running either in the past or in the future, we fail to acknowledge this happiness and cherish it while it exists.

Many mystics and spiritual guides have highlighted the importance of 'being in the present' because the present is said to be the moment of that divine power we refer to as God. Since time is created by human beings (an outcome of mental ability), it is not free and not godlike. It binds us in the mental knot and to break this knot, the spiritual well wishers motivate us to focus on the present. When they say 'everything is in the present', it doesn't mean that you will get a Jaguar, a holiday in Maldives and a Rs 400 crore lottery in this moment. When they say 'everything is in the moment', they refer to the mental and emotional peace, the inner happiness that we crave to experience as human beings. Being in the moment helps you experience the moments of peace and joy that keeps your whole being alive. It enables you to look at life as a whole and not in parts – work, personal, past, future. Being in the moment gives you a sense of awareness of your existence. It helps you understand that your past and your future are your mind's construct and in reality, in the present, you are always free from that bondage. This sense of mental peace strengthens your inner being and helps you to let yourself enjoy what you already have rather than rushing to get something that you wish you could have.

Mindfulness is regarded as one of the most powerful tools to overcome stress caused in multiple areas of our life. It is regarded as a vital practice to ease the ego and calm the mind, thus leading to more productivity, peace of mind and a joyous sense of being alive. It is also being employed in psychology to help patients deal with mental, emotional and/or physical complications such as anxiety, insomnia, anger issues, substance abuse, depression and so on.

Practical ways and benefits:

- Power of Breathing:

"Breath is the bridge which connects life to consciousness, which unites your body to your thoughts. Whenever your mind becomes scattered, use your breath as the means to take hold of your mind again." – Thich Nhat Hanh

Breath is regarded as the most powerful tool that helps in ending the mental and emotional scattering. When we get rambling thoughts and we instruct ourselves, 'Stop thinking', we begin to think on those lines all the more. It is just like this – Someone says, "don't think of a strawberry" and the moment you hear this, you get an image of a strawberry which stays in your head for at least fifteen seconds. Thus, the best and most effective way to disconnect from our thoughts and feelings related to past and future, is to bring the focus back to present by focusing on your breath. Breath is very effective in helping us get grounded in the present moment.

Breathing is something that we all do all the time and yet we are almost all the time unaware of this. To begin experiencing the power of breathing, start by bringing your focus on your breath. Just notice it. Don't try to control it, make it right or analyze it in any way. Just observe it. Become aware of it without any attempt to change it in any way. Notice the rise and fall of your chest or abdomen. Notice how long or short or deep or shallow is your breath. Let each cell of our body experience how it feels to breathe. Notice other physical tingling sensations in your body, if any.

Again, the focus is on just observing it and not controlling or analyzing it in any form. Notice how it feels to breathe. You can practice this anywhere and at any given time - while sitting in office, walking, before sleeping, cooking, eating etc. The more you practice it, the more you will become aware of your breath and its effects on your body, mind and inner being. While you practice breathing in awareness, there will be times where your mind will wander and take you to either the past or future. Don't worry, it is OK to experience this wandering and this does not mean that you are not being good at what you are doing or you are practicing it the wrong way. Notice how your mind keeps wandering every now and then and each time you become aware of these distractions, acknowledge and accept it and bring your focus back to your breath.

The more you practice breathing in awareness, the more you will feel liberated and firmly grounded in the present moment.

- What am I doing right now?

"Walk as if you are kissing the earth with your feet" – Thich Nhat Hanh

Any action that you do throughout the day, do it in awareness. Use all your five senses to focus on the activity that you are doing – be it walking in the park or exercising or eating or driving back from work.

In his book, *The Miracle of Mindfulness,* Thich Nhat Hanh talks about the importance of focusing on the action and being completely aware of the task at hand. He says, "While washing the dishes one should only be washing the dishes, which means that while washing the dishes one should be completely aware of the fact that one is washing the dishes. At first glance, that might seem a little silly: why put so much stress on a simple thing? But that's precisely the point."

Being aware of your actions at this moment helps you become aware of your existence and get further grounded in the present. It brings in your awareness the fact that you are alive at this very moment. And this realization of 'being alive' is extremely powerful in encouraging you to live every moment in peace and happiness. When you burn your finger with hot water or fire, you become completely aware of the pain caused by the burning. You can feel it in every sense of your being and it suddenly becomes the sole feeling of your existence. Now imagine the same principle being applied when you become completely aware of your present moment which isn't attached with any toxic experiences of feelings but pure joy and bliss. Imagine this bliss being the sole feeling of your existence. That is the power which the present moment holds. And this is why practicing mindfulness is challenging and almost unacceptable to human intellectual mind.

Practicing mindfulness has its own perks that sometimes become hard to describe, but it is a delight to experience. The more you practice it, the more you will discover its importance and relevance to your life. Be mindful every moment of your life because it is this feeling of being alive that will make you fall in love with your existence and become the profound source of boundless happiness.

20 Looking Inside Through Meditation

"The thing about Meditation is: You become more and more you."

~ David Lynch

When I was younger than I am today, I always perceived meditation as some alien trance world that mystics enter which is beyond human capacity. I always felt that in order to be able to meditate, you have got to leave the worldly life and embrace the spiritual world. It always existed in duality - either the worldly pleasures or the life of celibacy. The whole notion of 'meditation' was so grandiose that it almost seemed beyond my capacity to comprehend and further practice the same – sitting in a prescribed position, shooing away all your thoughts, concentrating on the divine light and not thinking of your feelings, experiences etc. How on earth would someone do that? I was a teenager with constant chaos in every cell of my body and to me, it seemed foolish to even try calming this hurricane within and become peaceful. The moment I would close my eyes, I would begin to feel anxious. Sitting with my eyes closed, even for a minute, neither made sense nor was it doable. I had tough times fighting with my mind to stop thinking every time I closed my eyes. I gave up meditation. I gave up the technique of meditation but not my quest to understand the Divinity (aka God).

To feed this quest, I began to seek knowledge in anything and everything – I would seek it in a book I was reading or a person I was meeting, a client I was counselling, the love and care I was experiencing, the nature, the perfect smiles of perfect strangers etc. Everything around me became like this giant library where I would just have to look at something and ask that question about divinity and I would get a hint – not the answers but the hint. And this hint was in the form of a 'feeling' which made me feel calm and happy. I began to do this unconsciously even when I was working and spending fourteen hours a day at office. This quest further diverted me to reading and I came across fascinating books that helped me understand the concept of divinity in a much simpler way.

This quest helped me understand that meditation is just one of the ways. To me, it is not the only way. The moment I derived this understanding, I came a step closer to feeling less burdened and more hopeful. For years I read and talked to some friends on this topic but it was only until recently that I began to practice it in my everyday life. I did not start with sitting cross-legged with my eyes closed, chanting a mantra and behaving as if I am opening the gates for some divine light to ascend through my head and fill my body with white light. NO. I began with changing my whole definition of meditation. Earlier it seemed like a stage where you feel at peace and divine within only when you reach that stage of being enlightened, after years of mediation. But now, I have come to understand that you can still feel at peace and divine without spending hours into meditation. Meditation to me is being able to stay connected with yourself every second of your life – while working, while washing the dishes, while cooking or anything – it is to become aware of your existence. This is the core of any meditation practice. It is what Zakir Hussain says in a documentary, *The Speaking Hand*[6], "When I play music, I pay homage. When I practice music, I meditate…"

Pre- Meditation, my way:

This is how I managed to climb the ladder of getting closer to Divinity:

a) I began to spend more time with myself. Doing the things I loved to do with complete awareness. I began to draw, after ten years, and write, for the very first time. While I did this, I began to let myself enjoy the whole process rather than jumping to a conclusion of whether it will turn out good or bad. Each time I would get critical thoughts (which happened almost every five minutes), I would remind myself about that one minute of peace I felt within when I held the pen or a pencil. I let that critical voice be and I continued to write and draw. I did not share what I was doing with anyone, for at least a month, because it was for me. It was for me to connect with my own inner self. And the more I practiced this, I more I felt closer to myself. It was as if I was encountering this side of myself which I never knew existed. That was the beginning of me getting in touch with myself.

b) I made a list of things that I love to do – drawing,

writing, helping others, dancing, listening to music etc and I began to incorporate this more and more in my everyday life. Be it for just five or twenty minutes a day, I did it. I began to get in touch with that feeling I experienced while I did what I loved to do. It was a combination of everything – peace, happiness, sense of relaxation. This doesn't mean all my miseries and sorrows disappeared. They were very much there and would continue to haunt me, but I still continued to take these baby steps.

c) When I shifted to Pune, a friend introduced me to the concept of 'being in the moment'. When I heard it, it seemed like a task I could never accomplish. Then I let myself practice it. Every day. Each time I remembered to be in the moment and 'doing what I was doing', I began to practice staying in the present moment.

d) I came across the concept of conscious breathing. Breathing in awareness. I reminded myself every minute that I am breathing. Just bringing my focus and attention to my breath. Not controlling it, not changing it but just noticing it. Noticing how slow or fast it is; the rise and fall of the stomach. Just being aware of it. Breath is the most powerful tool that helps you disconnect form the rambling chaotic mind. It is said to be the chain that connects your physical being to your spiritual being.

e) I joined yoga and began to practice every posture in awareness. They say that any exercise (especially yoga) should be an effortless effort. It is to bring your mind and body in synchrony. So each time I practiced yoga, my instructor would remind me to breathe and bring my focus back to my body and my mat.

After practicing all this for almost a year, I realized that everything I did gave me a feeling of being at peace. I had not practiced meditation; all that I had heard and read was that a person feels blissful, happy and at peace during and after meditation. I was feeling this feeling by doing all of the above. I began to smile more and to my surprise, the intensity with which my chaotic thoughts used to trouble me began to decrease. I began to experience more gratitude, more compassion and felt a lot closer to myself than I ever did. To me, that became an act of meditating. However, this isn't the end. This doesn't mean that you are done and now you no more have to sit cross-legged and pray to some Divine force. It means that you are now prepared to ascend to the next stage without feeling much anxious and threatened by the techniques of meditating.

Meditation is an art of experiencing something that your inner self desires and yearns to experience. And this yearning does not have an end. It is the process that enlivens you more. The more you learn, the more you wish to grow. This feeling of peace, happiness and calmness that is experienced in a meditative state is highly contagious. You reach a point where sitting for meditation doesn't become a task but it becomes a 'me time' and a 'happiness time'. It is as good as holding that brush and yearning to paint the canvas. It is as good as seeing an instrument and already hearing the tune in your mind. The only difference in that and the meditative state is that the feeling you experience in the latter form stays with your forever, growing and multiplying with time.

Begin this journey by asking yourself, "What do I want to do in my life?" instead of telling yourself, "What am I doing with my life!" List down as many things as you can think of and start doing that. Your mind will give you a thousand reasons or excuses of how you cannot do that. Don't let your excuses win over your desire to be happy. Your answer to the question itself is a step forward. Nobody else can take that step for you but yourself. So take those steps and begin your journey forward. Once you begin to do what you love to do, connect yourself with your existence by being in the moment and focusing on your breath. Become aware of your breathing every single second. Once you feel comfortable practicing this, go a step forward and allow yourself to sit in meditation. This is what I began to do and it worked for me, so you can go ahead and try this method, but remember this isn't the *only* method that would work for you. It is your quest. Look for other ways which would work for you. Keep that inner-quest going and you would soon find yourself in love with the whole concept of meditation.

Simple methods to begin Meditation:

Buy yourself an alarm clock if you don't have any. If you don't have an alarm at home, put a timer in your mobile. Start with putting a timer for two minutes. For those two minutes, close your eyes, sit cross legged (preferably, sit on a pillow or a yoga blog where your knees almost touch the floor) and put your hands on your knees with your palms facing up. If you have many people around in the house, look for a place where there would be no one to disturb you or excuse yourself to have a room to you for that period. In those two minutes, focus your attention on your breath and bring your attention to your body.

Notice how your body feels and how your mind is forcing you to get out of this posture by either giving you a slight headache or a backache or by simply creating thoughts of someone coming in. Stay with it. Do not open your eyes. Each time you feel distracted, notice the distraction and bring yourself back to your breath. Notice if your heartbeat and your breath is calmer and deeper or rapid and anxious. Just notice it and stay with it without trying to control it or calming it. If chanting helps, you can chant your mantras in your mind. You can also try various popular breathing techniques[7] to get grounded. Open your eyes only when the timer goes off. Do this as often as you can, preferably every day. Once you begin to get comfortable keeping your eyes closed and bringing your focus and attention to the inside, increase the time to five minutes. Each time you get comfortable with the set time, increase the time by two or five minutes.

Remember:

You are already a spiritual being. The whole idea of attaining the spiritual level makes us believe that we have two selves – the physical body and the spiritual one which is lost in universal abyss and we need to find and bring it back to feel whole and complete. This struggle can also be felt while you sit to meditate. Notice that initially your mind would want to control and take charge of things and you would constantly find yourself looking for something beyond. That's your mind playing tricks. The energy and divinity is within you. The candle is already there with the match box beside it. All you got to do is be present every day to light the candle. While you light a candle, you don't wait or struggle to see the light, right? It is just there.

Meditation is an art of lighting that candle which ironically is already lit. Let yourself feel the light every single second, and not just at the time of meditation. Make every minute of your life a meditation, a divine dance and that is when you will fall in love with yourself and your life all over again.

21 | Embrace your Body, Mind and Soul

"The universe is one being. Everything and everyone is interconnected through invisible web of stories. Whether we are aware of it or not, we are all in a silent conversation. Do no harm. Practice compassion. And do not gossip behind anyone's back – not even a seemingly innocent remark! The words that come out of our mouth do not vanish but are perpetually stored in infinite space, and they will come back to us in due time. One man's pain will hurt us all. One man's joy will make everyone happy"

~ Elif Shafak, The Forty Rules of Love

I always looked at these three aspects of my being as three separate powerful entities that possessed the ability to be both constructive and/or destructive. It was only when I began to practice Yoga that I understood how these three aren't separate parts of me but an intertwined chain of Body Mind Soul that make my whole being a single powerful entity. Once you understand the concept of embracing Body Mind Soul, you begin to feel lighter, calmer and more in connect with your Self.

The body, mind and soul work as a team exchanging and sharing the divine energy within. The profusion or restriction of this energy flow determines our state of being. When we are in alignment with our body, mind and soul, we feel begin to experience joy in everything that we do, and become more loving and compassionate and capable of creating a life that we want.

Body

"Weight loss does not make people happy or peaceful. Being thin does not address the emptiness that has no shape or weight or name. Even a wildly successful diet is a colossal failure because inside the new body is the same sinking heart." - Geneen Roth

We almost always find faults with our physical body. In several cultures, the perfection of physical beauty is given prime importance. Hence, from a very young age, we begin to get obsessed with perfecting our already perfect physical body. We all almost get convinced that the way we look and our physical appearance is not right. We begin to blindly follow the definition of 'perfect physical beauty' created by society and challenge ourselves to fit in that category of being 'beautiful'. Instead of teaching how to embrace our body the way it is, we are taught, at every step, to change our perfectly gifted physical being. The obsession has reached a stage where illusionary beauty symbols - in the form of several beauty pageants, television advertisements - are created, which give the message that if your body doesn't fit into this description of perfection; you have, by default, become less of a human being. Thus, teenagers begin to center their entire time, energy and focus in grooming themselves to fit in this 'beauty' clan. Due to this conditioning, we are never trained or taught to embrace our natural physical being, leading to identity crises and several physical and mental disorders.

Your body, the way it is, is perfect in its existence. Words like thin, fat, white, black, perfect shape, six packs, thin waist etc are all created by society. In reality, there is no such thing as categories of physical beauty. Your body is created for a purpose – to help you unite with your spiritual being. Your body doesn't have the purpose of looking as beautiful as you can, but that of being as healthy as you can. Denying your body the way it is, is like abandoning your core self and struggling to replace it with someone else's self. The moment you deny your physical being, the way your natural body looks, you begin to make more space for 'disease' within. And this disease doesn't get cured with diets, mindless exercises to reduce/gain weight, beauty products etc. Even if you manage to come close to the definition of perfection, there will be a void inside which will continue to call out to tell you that you still lack something.

Your body communicates with you all the time. Find time to listen to it. Your body knows it all. If you don't treat it well (feeding it protein or carbs or all possible junk or starving it for days), it will communicate the unease in the form of pain or illness or weight gain/loss. Your body is *you*; it needs love, care and nurturing. It needs you to embrace it the way it is made and works towards maintaining its health (not shape). It is your prime duty to keep it healthy. Not beautiful, but healthy. When I say healthy, I mean to keep it at ease and not bring it closer to disease. When you embrace your physical being the way it is made, you begin to make peace with it. It is the most vital step towards bringing balance in your body.

Once you embrace it and fill it with love and care, it becomes the most powerful vessel of containing the powerful life force or the divine energy. Your body is your connect with mind and soul and its primary task is to stay united with the mind and soul to complete the spectrum of your existence. As rightly said by Neale Donald Walsch, "If you think your life is about *doingness*, you do not understand what you are about. Your soul doesn't care what you do for a living-and when your life is over, neither will you. Your soul cares only about what you're *being* while you're doing whatever you're doing. It is a state of *beingness* the soul is after, not a state of doingness."

Mind

When you inhale your first breath, your mind begins its journey of losing its purity. It is a membrane which begins to fill up with beliefs, experiences, feelings, thoughts and thus begin its journey of taking your entire being towards chaos, fear, anxiety, shame, guilt and further away from inner happiness. Embracing your mind is challenging because you cannot journey back and erase all that has been accumulated in your mind. But you can certainly journey forward by embracing all that is (your past experiences, feelings, thoughts, future inhibitions and so on) and become an observer of the mind. This can be done by listening to the voice inside your head as often as you can. Pay special attention to repetitive thoughts, feelings that you continue to play inside your head over and over and over again. By doing this, you begin to watch the 'thinker' which is similar to listening to the voice in your head. When you begin to observe this thought pattern, try to listen to it without analyzing it – without categorizing it as good, bad, right or wrong.

If 'watching the thinker' feels more challenging, you can practice noticing your thoughts and at the same time, bringing your attention back to your breath to be in 'here and now'. Continue your focus on your breath and notice the kind of thoughts your mind creates. You will be amazed and at the same time, amused by its ability to drag you aimless in some random direction and try in every manner to make you feel fearful, insecure, guilty and anxious. Maintaining the focus in here and now will help you stay grounded in the 'present' moment and create a no-mind space in which you will be thinking and alert, but your mind will stay in the 'here and now'.

Always remember that you are not your mind. Your mind is a vital component of your being. Embrace it not just in running the materialistic rat race but also in fulfilling the meaning of your existence. When you succeed in doing that, you reach a state of ecstasy where bliss and love becomes the source of your being.

Soul

'The word 'enlightenment' conjures up the idea of some superhuman accomplishment, and the ego likes to keep it that way, but it is simply your natural state of felt oneness with Being.' – Eckhart Tolle

Since we are gifted with intellect, we love to analyze and understand everything related to our existence through this intellect. We begin to look for a theory or validations that make sense to our conscious mind. Anything that we feel within, which fails to make sense to this conscious mind is discarded by the intellect. We wish to know (intellectually) what soul looks like, what the divine force shapes like. We begin to give it a name, a form, a voice, an identity that makes sense to our conscious mind. This is just a trap that we create for ourselves, leading us not closer but away from the divine life force.

If you wish to embrace the soul or divine aspect of your being,

- Listen to your Body: It will tell you 'who you are'.
- Listen to your Mind by being an observer to your thought patterns: It will tell you what you can become.
- Journey inwards by being in the 'here and now': It will tell you what your existence is all about.

The words like soul, God, Divine Light, Life force or Qi etc are just created to intellectually understand our existence. Instead of spending time in understanding these words and concepts, spend your time in living and getting closer to this force. Feeling its presence is more important than understanding its presence. The presence of this soul can be felt when you divert your attention inwards to your body and mind. The divine force is integrated in your body and mind and embracing all three is to recognize the divine light (God) within. It isn't a road map for just a mystic or a monk or a Sufi or a man who is on a spiritual journey. You may be a businessman or a sportsman or a doctor or an engineer or an artist but you are a human being to begin with and embracing your body, mind and soul becomes your primary goal by default.

TRYING TO ACHIEVE TOTAL HARMONY OF MIND, BODY AND CASHFLOW.

Role of Yoga in embracing Body, Mind and Soul

Yoga in Sanskrit means 'Union'. The aim of yoga is to realize one's True Self as the source of happiness. It is an art that teaches you to harmonize your body, mind and soul to feel the presence of that divinity within. The *asanas* are designed to help you embrace your physical, mental and spiritual being.

When you begin to practice yoga, you begin to become consciously aware of your 'self' by bringing your focus and attention to your body and the mat. It helps you get grounded in the 'here and now' and strengthens your ability to get in touch with your body. It enables you to listen to your body and helps you accept it the way it is. It teaches you to make peace with your body by not torturing it to get the perfect pose but to respect, love and care the physical sheath of your Being. In my yoga practice, my instructor taught me that it isn't important to attain the 'right' shape, it is important to embrace and treasure the shape that you already have. When I would struggle to get that perfect posture, she would point out my struggle of not being who I am but wanting to become someone else. When I began to develop my relationship with my body by beginning to embrace it the way it is, I began to feel a deep sense of grace and satisfaction within.

While practicing yoga, my instructor taught me to do every *asana* in mindfulness. Transitioning from one posture to another, the key was to continue the focus and attention on the body (or the body-mat contact). The times my mind would go astray with constant rambling thoughts, I would lose balance. The resulting frustration turns into a smile when you become an observer to your own thought patterns. Thus, while doing yoga, you begin to learn to calm your mind and at the same time make peace with your physical being. This sense of bliss is nothing but recognition of the life force within.

The more you begin to practice the art of Yoga, the more you expand the divine force within and that is when your existence becomes the sole reason and the source of boundless happiness which you continue to feel in every breath of your life.

***

Message to all my "happy" readers

When I began writing this book, all I had in mind was just one goal – to touch other lives through my writing. With that thought, I started jotting down what I felt, knew and had experienced regarding the feeling called happiness. These 21 ways are close to my heart because they taught me how to look at happiness from a less intimidating angle. Since happiness is a very relative term, these 21 ways *cannot* be the *only* universal ways leading to happiness. We all have different perceptions and hence, it becomes almost necessary to dwell within and seek what is best for our living. There is no perfect formula for happiness. We need to seek our own little pleasures and indulge in them.

These ways are not thumb rules for you, but ideas that you would like to implement and work your way through to what suits you best. Keep on asking yourself – what is it that makes me truly happy? The journey of asking and practicing it is important. This book is my attempt to fuel that urge, that desire to be happy that we all carry within our hearts. Take this moment as an opportunity and promise yourself *that* happiness which you truly deserve. Make an effort to keep yourself happy and give yourself a hug when things get tough. We all have days when we feel sad and crappy, but also moments when we're at our happiest. Together, these moments make life. You are a magnificent existence on this planet and even if you deny it, this universal truth remains unchanged.

My favourite Sufi poet Rumi says, "Your task is not to seek for love, but merely to seek and find all the barriers within yourself that you have built against it." To me, happiness and love are just two sides of a coin. Just like we build barriers around to stop love from entering our lives, we also develop these same barriers to keep happiness away. We all have issues and we will always have challenges in life, but it is up to us to decide if we want to give in to the excuses or rather take baby steps towards filling our heart with love and happiness. It is convenient to brood over how our life, personal and professional, is in a mess. You will always feel that the other person who seems happy has a smooth sail in life, but know that people who look happy chose to not let themselves drown in their miseries. They decided to endure the difficulties and ascend to their highest potential. We all have a choice – a choice to ascend or descend to our highest potential. What we choose, becomes a part of the mystery we call destiny.

Allow yourself to be happy – today, tomorrow and every single day of your conscious life. I pray to God to give each and every one of you the ability to embrace happiness and make your life the best gift not just for yourselves but also for everyone around. Spread this happiness bug in your life as well as in the lives of people around and that is when you will begin to see the beauty of your existence. That is when you will experience how wonderful it is to live in harmony with your fellow human beings.

God bless us.

Notes

1. *Defence mechanism*: Coping mechanism that people use to distance themselves from an unpleasant situation – used to fight anxiety and stress.

2. *Common defences*: Listed by Sigmund Freud as ego defences; part of defence mechanisms.

   a) Denial: Refusal to accept the reality because it is more painful and anxiety-provoking, and believing that the situation or feeling does not exist.

   b) Repression: Forcing, hiding, or blocking hurtful feelings, thoughts, impulses from the consciousness, putting them in the unconscious because those are socially/morally unacceptable.

   c) Displacement: When thoughts, feelings and impulses directed at one person or object are taken out upon another person or object instead of the one that caused hurt.

   d) Regression: Regressing back into an early state of mental/physical development which is more safe, secure and comforting than the present reality.

3. *I am OK, You are not OK:* A well-known Psychologist Eric Berne formulated four basic

positions termed under Transactional Analysis, one of the theories of Psychology. According to him, human beings operate from the following four life positions in their lives:

a. I am OK, You are OK – Healthy, Assertive nature, wise adult.

b. I am OK, You are not OK – People who generally play the Blame Game; have a 'poor you' or arrogant attitude towards others.

c. I am not OK, You are OK – Individuals who drown themselves in self-pity; act or feel helpless; pessimists; can easily be taken for granted; love to be a doormat.

d. I am not OK, You are not OK – Worst life position. These are people who feel they are good for nothing and even others around are equally useless.

4. Read the book Why Men Don't Listen and Women Can't Read Maps by Allen and Barbara Pease to learn more about such differences in men and women.

5. In the book *The Forty Rules of Love,* author Elif Shafak describes rules of love as given by a famous Sufi Dervish, Shams of Tabriz. This is the 28th Rule from the list of 40.

6. *The Speaking Hand* by Sumantra Ghosal: A documentary film on Zakir Hussain and the art of playing Tabla. It showcases Zakir Hussain's growth from the by-lanes of Bombay to his

current fame as a world famous Tabla player.

7. *Breathing techniques:* Different ways of practicing breathing for relaxation and good health:

   a. Anulom Vilom – One of the most effective pranayama (breathing exercises) to purify the mind and body. Keeping your right thumb on the right nostril, breathe in and then closing the left nostril with last two fingers of the right hand, breathe out. Repeat the process for a few minutes, inhaling and exhaling deeply.

   b. Bhramari – Cover your ears with your index fingers or thumbs. Take a deep breath in (inhale) and exhale it out with a humming sound like a bee. Repeat it 5-6 times and get back to normal breathing. Observe the sensations in your body and feel the quietness within. Once you feel fine, repeat the bhramari pranayama, gradually extending the number.

   c. Om chant - Sit in Padmasana (the basic cross-legged yoga posture), close your eyes and bring your focus to your breath. Once you are seated comfortably, join your hands in the prayer position, keeping your eyes closed. Take a deep breath in, fill your belly completely and exhale out slowly, with an audible chant of 'Om' synced with your breath.

References

1. The Miracle of Mindfulness, Thich Nhat Hanh; Random House UK; 2008

2. Practicing The Power of Now, Eckhart Tolle; Yogi Impressions; 2002

3. Conversations with God, An Uncommon Dialogue - Book I, Neale Donald Walsch; Putnam Adult; 1995

4. Siddhartha, Hermann Hesse; New Directions (U.S.)' 1922, 1951 (U.S.)

5. The Forty Rules of Love, Elif Shafak; Penguin UK; 2011

6. Illusions - The Adventures of a Reluctant Messiah, Richard Bach; Dell Publishing Co., Inc.; 1977